Civil War Texas

CIVIL WAR TEXAS

A History and a Guide

By Ralph A. Wooster

TEXAS STATE
HISTORICAL ASSOCIATION

Library of Congress Cataloging-in-Publication Data

Wooster, Ralph A.
    Civil War Texas : a history and a guide / by Ralph A. Wooster.
        p.   cm.   — (Fred Rider Cotten popular history series; no. 14)
    Includes bibliographical references (p.   ).
    ISBN 0-87611-171-1 (alk. paper)
    1. Texas—History—Civil War, 1861–1865. 2. Historic sites—Texas—
    Guidebooks. 3. Texas—Guidebooks. I. Title. II. Series.
    E532.W66 1999
    976.4'05—dc21   98-56282
                                                                                          CIP

Number fourteen in the Fred Rider Cotten Popular History Series.

Published by the Texas State Historical Association in cooperation with the Center
for Studies in Texas History at the University of Texas at Austin.

Cover photograph tinted by David Timmons.

Cover: Col. Julius A. Andrews, Thirty-second Texas Cavalry Regiment. *Photograph
courtesy Lawrence T. Jones III, Austin.*

CONTENTS

Two members of the Twenty-seventh Cavalry Regiment (also known as First Texas Legion), Ross's Brigade. *Courtesy Lawrence T. Jones III, Austin.*

1.
THE WAR BEGINS

ON FEBRUARY 1, 1861, delegates to the Texas state convention, called to consider federal relations, passed by a vote of 166 to 8, an ordinance separating Texas from the United States. Declaring that the federal government was using its power as a weapon against the Southern people, the secession ordinance repealed the annexation ordinance of 1845 by which Texas joined the American Union. The measure provided that the act of secession would be submitted to the people for ratification or rejection on February 23. If ratified in the popular election the ordinance would become effective on March 2, 1861, the twenty-fifth anniversary of the Texas Declaration of Independence from Mexico.[1]

Passage of the secession ordinance, and its subsequent ratification by the voters on February 23, came after several years of controversy over the issues of slavery and states' rights. The election of Abraham Lincoln as President, on a platform pledged to halt the expansion of slavery in the territories, convinced many Southerners that separation from the Union was necessary. In December 1860, South Carolina seceded. The next month Mississippi, Florida, Alabama, Georgia, and Louisiana held conventions which took similar action. Texas governor Sam Houston opposed calling a convention in Texas, but a group of prominent citizens led by O. M. Roberts, John S. "Rip" Ford, and William P. Rogers issued a call for a convention to consider the issue of federal relations. Elections

"Surrender of Ex-General Twiggs . . . to the Texan Troops in the Gran Plaza," San Antonio, February 16, 1861. From *Harper's Weekly*, March 23, 1861. *Photograph courtesy Jerry Thompson, Laredo.*

for delegates took place in early January, and on January 28 the convention—which included as delegates former governor Hardin R. Runnels, four future governors, and seven future Confederate generals—began its deliberations in Austin. The following day the delegates passed by a vote of 152 to 6 a resolution stating that it was the sense of the convention that "Texas should separately secede from the Union." Three days later the convention adopted the secession ordinance.[2]

After the ratification of secession by the voters in late February, the state convention adopted a measure uniting Texas with the newly formed Confederate States of America. Governor Houston, though he had reluctantly accepted the voters' approval of secession, refused to recognize the authority of the convention to take such action. When Houston declined to take an oath of allegiance to the Confederacy, the convention declared the office of governor vacant and made Lt. Gov. Edward Clark, who took the oath, governor.[3]

Even before Houston was removed from office, the Committee of Public Safety created by the convention took steps to secure the surrender of federal property in Texas. The committee appointed commissioners to negotiate with Brig. Gen. David E. Twiggs, commander of United States troops in Texas, whose headquarters were in San Antonio. Twiggs, a Georgian with forty-eight years of military service, was sympathetic with Texas but had not received orders from federal authorities concerning the matter. After several days of fruitless negotiations, the committee instructed Ben McCulloch, a veteran Texas Ranger and Mexican War hero, to lead several hundred Texas volunteers into San Antonio to demand the surrender of federal property. Before dawn on February 16, McCulloch and his troops rode into the Alamo city and took Twiggs into custody. Wishing to avoid bloodshed, Twiggs agreed to turn over federal property provided that his troops be allowed to retain their sidearms and march to the coast for exit out of the state.[4]

THEN AND NOW

The modern city of Austin, with a population of half a million, little resembles the Civil War town of thirty-five hundred inhabitants where the Secession Convention met. The convention held its sessions in the House of Representatives chambers on the second floor of the state capitol building. The white limestone building, dedicated in 1853, no longer stands. It burned on November 9, 1881, in a fire starting in an improperly installed woodstove. The present capitol building was constructed on the same site at the north end of Congress Avenue. Historical markers on the capitol grounds at North Congress and West 1st Street commemorate the Secession Convention and Austin's role in the Civil War.

Visitors to the capitol grounds can see the Austin Confederate Monument, Hood's Texas Brigade Monument, and Terry's Texas Rangers Memorial. Statues of Albert Sidney Johnston, Jefferson Davis, John H. Reagan, and Robert E. Lee are on the South Mall of the University of Texas campus. The Texas State Cemetery, located between 7th and 11th Streets, is the burial place for seven Civil War generals from Texas. A bronze portrait bust of John A. Wharton and a carved marble figure of Albert Sidney Johnston designed by renowned sculptor Elisabet Ney mark their grave sites in the cemetery.

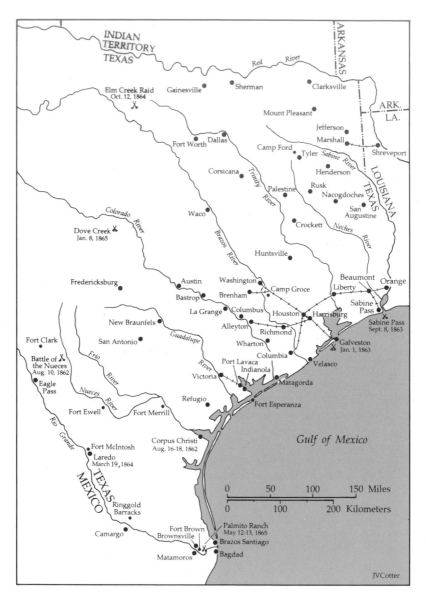

Texas. *Map by John V. Cotter.*

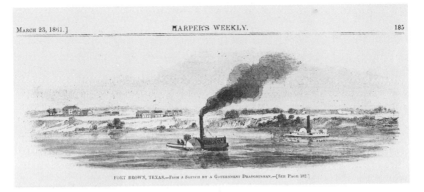

FORT BROWN, TEXAS.—From a Sketch by a Government Draughtsman.—[See Page 182.]

"Fort Brown, Texas," abandoned by U.S. troops in March 1861; occupied by Texas troops. From *Harper's Weekly*, March 23, 1861. *CN 10125. Courtesy Prints and Photographs Collection, Center for American History, University of Texas at Austin.*

The Committee of Public Safety authorized the recruiting of volunteer troops in the spring of 1861. In Central Texas Col. Henry E. McCulloch, younger brother of Ben McCulloch, recruited ten companies which became the First Texas Mounted Rifles, later known as the First Texas Cavalry Regiment. McCulloch's cavalry was assigned duty in north central Texas taking the surrender of federal property there. John S. "Rip" Ford took command of a regiment of volunteers in the Houston area known as the Second Texas Mounted Rifles, or Second Texas Cavalry. Ford was ordered to the lower Rio Grande, where he occupied Fort Brown and took possession of other federal property.[5]

The firing on Fort Sumter in April 1861, followed by calls from President Davis for volunteers, spurred recruitment efforts in Texas. Governor Clark divided the state into military districts headed by prominent Texans who assisted in recruiting and organizing troops. There was little difficulty in enrolling men in the cavalry as most Texans preferred the mounted service. Lt. Col. Arthur Fremantle of the British Coldstream Guards, who visited the state during the war, observed that "it was found very difficult to raise infantry in Texas, as no Texan walks a yard if he can help it." As a result two-thirds of the twenty-five thousand Texans recruited in 1861 were in cavalry regiments.[6]

Outfitting these new regiments often proved more difficult than recruiting them. Many of the men furnished their own weapons, resulting in a wide variety that included hunting rifles and muskets, shotguns, old flintlock muskets, ancient fowling pieces, and expensive silverplated handguns. Bowie knives, Colt revolvers, and even lances were carried by some Texans.

Some weapons, particularly artillery pieces, were obtained from federal forts occupied by state and Confederate troops. Both state and Confederate governments appointed agents to purchase weapons abroad, but lack of hard currency and the federal blockade of the Southern coastline made their tasks difficult. Various facilities were constructed in Texas for the manufacture of weapons and ammunition. A major ordnance works built near Tyler produced thousands of rifles, cartridges, musket balls, ammunition boxes, and canteens. Other ordnance works were established in Anderson, Austin, Bastrop, Bexar, Brazoria, Calhoun, Cherokee, Dallas, Galveston, Harris, Harrison, Marion, Rusk, and Travis Counties. The Confederate Army later opened a number of shops and depots in Texas for the manufacture, repair, and distribution of clothing, shoes, wagons, and other materials of war. Convicts at the state penitentiary at Huntsville turned out thousands of yards of cloth each day for use in Confederate and state uniforms.[7]

Training for the new recruits varied. In the spring of 1861 Governor Clark set up military camps in several locations. Some of these, such as Camp Berlin near Brenham, Camp Cypress in northeast Harris County, Camp Honey Springs near Dallas, and Camp Roberts in Smith County, were primarily mustering stations. Others, such as Camp Bosque near Waco, Camp Clark on the San Marcos River, and Camp Van Dorn on Buffalo Bayou, were larger camps where instruction was received. Near Hempstead two camps, Groce and Hébert, were across the road from each other. Even in these camps the training consisted primarily of rudimentary drill in marching and handling weapons. Much time was spent in socializing and in athletic contests. Harold Simpson, historian of one of Texas's most famous Civil War units, Hood's Texas Brigade, notes that the camp of the Fourth Texas Infantry near Roan's Prairie in Grimes County took on the aspects of summer

THEN AND NOW

The numerous camps established in Texas during the Civil War have disappeared. Markers prepared by the Texas Historical Commission indicate the location of some of the camps. Among these are markers in or near the towns of Ben Franklin (Camp Rusk), Bryan (Camp Speight), Gilmer (Camp Talley), Hempstead (Camps Groce and Hébert), and Victoria (Camp Henry E. McCulloch).

The various Civil War ordnance works have also disappeared. Again, historical markers provide information on the location and the activities of these establishments. Among these are the Austin C.S.A. marker at North Congress and West 1st Street, the Nash Iron Works marker twenty miles west of Jefferson on FM 729, the Marshall C.S.A. marker in the roadside park on US 80, the Confederate Gun Factory marker on US 84 in Rusk, and the Arsenal Magazine marker at 646 South Main in San Antonio.

Olympics as the men competed in running, jumping, boxing, and wrestling.[8]

The majority of Texans recruited for Confederate service spent the war west of the Mississippi River, defending the region from Indian raids and federal attacks. In May 1861, Col. William C. Young and the Eleventh Cavalry, recruited in North Texas, crossed the Red River and occupied federal forts in Indian Territory. In that same month Ben McCulloch was appointed brigadier general in the Confederate Army with orders to defend Arkansas and Indian Territory from Union incursion. In late summer, McCulloch, commanding the "Army of the West" consisting of the Third Texas Cavalry, the Fourth Arkansas Cavalry, and the Third Louisiana Infantry, moved into southwestern Missouri to support Sterling Price's Missouri Confederates. On August 10 the combined forces of McCulloch and Price defeated a small but well-disciplined Union Army commanded by Nathaniel Lyon at Oak Hill, or Wilson's Creek, near Springfield, Missouri.[9]

McCulloch's command was joined by other Texas units in the autumn of 1861. These included the Sixth Texas Cavalry led by Col. B. Warren Stone and including among its officers a young Texan already known for his exploits in Indian fighting, Lawrence

S. "Sul" Ross; Col. William C. Young's Eleventh Texas Cavalry; and a cavalry battalion commanded by Maj. John W. Whitfield. In the spring of 1862 McCulloch's troops, now a division in an army commanded by Maj. Gen. Earl Van Dorn, took part in the battle at Elkhorn Tavern, or Pea Ridge, in the northwestern corner of Arkansas. In this battle McCulloch was killed while reconnoitering the enemy's position. After the death of McCulloch and Col. James M. McIntosh, second-ranking officer in the division, Col. Elkanah Greer of the Third Texas assumed temporary command. The fighting continued the next morning but at midday General Van Dorn broke off the engagement and the Confederates retreated.[10]

At the time of McCulloch's death other Texans were attempting to gain control of New Mexico Territory for the Confederacy. In July 1861, the veteran frontiersman Lt. Col. John R. Baylor and units of the Second Texas Mounted Rifles moved into New Mexico and occupied the town of Mesilla. After defeating Union forces in the area, Baylor issued a proclamation creating the Confederate Territory of Arizona south of the Thirty-fourth Parallel, or roughly the southern half of present-day New Mexico and Arizona. Baylor assumed power as governor and made Mesilla his capital.[11]

Later that winter three regiments of Texas Confederate cavalry commanded by Brig. Gen. Henry H. Sibley moved into New Mexico. On February 21, 1862, Sibley's cavalry, led in battle by Texan Tom Green, defeated Union forces at Valverde near Fort Craig and moved up the Rio Grande to occupy Albuquerque and Santa Fe. In late March units of Sibley's army, led by the colorful Victoria poet-soldier William R. "Dirty Shirt" Scurry, defeated federal troops at Glorieta Pass in the mountains east of Santa Fe. Unfortunately for the Texans, during the course of the battle a Union detachment commanded by Maj. John M. Chivington swung around behind the Confederate lines and destroyed Scurry's wagon train containing badly needed food, ammunition, and medicine. The loss of the supply train was a serious blow to the Confederates. Sibley, faced with a shortage of supplies and having received reports of a major Union troop movement from California toward New Mexico, decided to retreat to Texas. His retreat ended operations in New Mexico and put an end to the Confederate territory of Arizona.[12]

Two weeks after Sibley's army began its withdrawal from New Mexico, Texas's most distinguished soldier, Albert Sidney Johnston, was killed at Shiloh. Johnston, former secretary of war in the Texas Republic and commander of the U.S. Second Cavalry in the 1850s, was the highest ranking field general in the Confederate Army. Appointed to command all Confederate forces in the western department by his old friend, Jefferson Davis, Johnston concen- trated a large army at Corinth, Mississippi, in late March in an effort to block the

Thomas Lubbock. *Courtesy J. Dale West Collection, Longview.*

advance of U. S. Grant's Union forces. On April 6, 1862, Johnston launched a major attack on Grant's army near a small country church in southwestern Tennessee called Shiloh. In the initial assault, Johnston's Confederates drove the federals back, but in the afternoon Johnston was hit by a bullet that severed the artery on his right leg. Within fifteen minutes Johnston bled to death. Under his successor, P. G. T. Beauregard, the Confederates continued fighting until dusk, but the next day Grant, who had been reinforced during the night, drove the Confederates back. On the evening of April 7 the defeated Confederates withdrew to Corinth.[13]

Three Texas regiments fought at Shiloh. The Second Texas infantry, consisting of ten companies recruited from the Houston and Central Texas areas commanded by Col. John C. Moore, was in the thick of fighting on the Confederate right on April 6. The Ninth Texas, a small infantry regiment made up of men from northeast Texas commanded by Col. Wright A. Stanley, was to the left of the Second Texas. The Ninth was under heavy enemy fire in the fighting on the 6th and suffered heavy casualties. The Eighth

Texas Cavalry, better known as Terry's Texas Rangers, attacked the enemy flanks in fighting on both the 6th and the 7th. Col. John A. Wharton, the wealthy Brazoria County planter who commanded the Rangers after the deaths of Benjamin F. Terry and Tom Lubbock the previous winter, was severely wounded but remained on the field until after the battle had ended. Capt. Ashbel Smith, the distinguished physician and diplomat who commanded Company C of the Second Texas, and Pvt. Sam Houston Jr., also of Company C, were also among the Texans wounded at Shiloh.[14]

Shiloh was the bloodiest battle of the first twelve months of the Civil War. With total Confederate and federal dead and wounded of twenty-three thousand men, there were more casualties at Shiloh than all the other battles of the first year of the war combined. Shiloh brought Texas and the South face to face with the grim reality of war.

Hispanic Confederates from Texas. *Courtesy Lawrence T. Jones III, Austin.*

2.
DEFENDING THE TEXAS COAST

THE CONFEDERATE defeats at Pea Ridge and Shiloh in the spring of 1862 discouraged some Texans who had believed the South would defeat the North in a few months. When enthusiasm for military service began to wane the Confederate Congress on April 16, 1862, passed the first of several conscription laws to assure that manpower needs of the army would be met. The conscription laws were generally unpopular in Texas and elsewhere but they did serve as a continued stimulant to recruitment as Southerners volunteered for service to avoid the odium of conscription.

The war came directly to Texas in the late spring of 1862 as the Union Navy became more active along the coast. A naval blockade of Texas seaports had begun the previous July when the Union warship *South Carolina* commanded by Capt. James Alden arrived off the coast near Galveston. During the next ten months a few blockade runners were captured, shots were exchanged between the *South Carolina* and Galveston batteries, and the Confederate patrol schooner *Royal Yacht* was burned, but no effort was made to occupy the city. In May 1862, Capt. Henry Eagle, master of the Union frigate *Santee*, demanded the surrender of Galveston. Maj. Gen. Paul O. Hébert, commanding Confederate forces in Texas, sensed that this was only a bluff and declined to surrender but did order the evacuation of civilians, livestock, and excessive provisions from the island. Although Captain Eagle was unable to enforce his surrender demands, his action caused concern to state and Confederate officials. Gov. Francis Lubbock was determined to defend the city against any possible attack, but General Hébert was of the opinion that because of its exposed position Galveston Island could not be held against a determined Union assault.[15]

The first serious effort to occupy a Texas port came not at Galveston but at Corpus Christi. In August 1862, Lt. John W. Kittredge, commanding a five-ship Union flotilla, attempted to capture the city. Confederate forces, organized and led by Maj. Alfred M. Hobby, a local merchant and state legislator, beat back two attacks on August 16. Two days later Kittredge resumed the effort, but the Confederates, protected by an old earthwork constructed by Gen. Zachary Taylor in 1845, held their shoreline position. In a final effort, Kittredge sent some of his seamen ashore with a field gun, but spirited charges by Hobby and his troops drove them back. Kittredge withdrew his men, but hoped to make another attempt to take the city later. In September he went ashore near Corpus at Flour Bluff to reconnoiter but was captured by Capt. John Ireland's company of Confederates.[16]

After the failure to take Corpus Christi, the federal navy turned its attention to the upper Texas coast. In late September 1862, three Union vessels commanded by Lt. Frederick Crocker crossed the bar at Sabine Pass and began shelling Fort Sabine, which had been constructed the previous year to defend the waterway separating Texas and Louisiana. After a brief exchange of artillery fire, the Confederates spiked their four cannons and evacuated the fort. Crocker's men came ashore, destroyed Fort Sabine, and burned the railway bridge over Taylor's Bayou and the railroad depot at Sabine Pass. On October 17, Crocker and his bluejackets came ashore again, this time burning fourteen barracks and stables west of Sabine Pass and driving off Confederate troops in the area before returning to their vessels. Meanwhile, local Confederates, fearful that the enemy might attempt to advance inland, completed construction of Fort Grigsby on the Neches River, near present-day Port Neches. A movement towards Beaumont was anticipated by the Confederates, but the Union military instead

THEN AND NOW

Corpus Christi was a town of twelve hundred people when the Civil War began. Many of the women and children moved out of town during the shelling by Kittredge's Union flotilla. They returned soon after the battle but many left again when the Union Navy bombarded the city in September 1863. Although the Union fleet controlled the harbor and federal scouting parties entered the city several times in the winter of 1863–64, the city was not occupied until the end of the war.

The Centennial House at 411 North Upper Broadway, the city's oldest building, constructed in 1849, was used as a hospital during the Civil War and may be visited today. A historical marker under the high bridge at the end of Water Street points out that Corpus Christi was used for blockade running early in the war. Another marker at FM 699 north of town at the bridge over the Nueces River notes that the old Matamoros Road which crossed the river there was used for the transportation of Texas cotton through Mexico during the war.

turned its attention to Galveston.[17]

Citizens of Galveston, the state's second-largest city, had been fearful of a Union attack since Captain Eagle's demand for surrender in May. General Hébert, convinced that defense of the city was impossible, ordered the removal of all heavy cannon, except one at Fort Point at the mouth of the harbor, from the island to the mainland. Therefore, when Union Commander William B. Renshaw brought a flotilla of four ships into the harbor on October 4 there was little the Confederates could do. After a four-day truce to allow civilian evacuation, Galveston was surrendered on October 8, an event described by prominent island attorney William Pitt Ballinger as "a bleak day in our history."[18]

Although his superiors were pleased that Galveston had surrendered, Commander Renshaw was worried. He had only 150 men with which to occupy the island and was fearful that the Confederates might counterattack. From informers he heard that John B. Magruder, the newly appointed Confederate commander of Texas, intended to retake the island. Magruder, known to friends in the old army as "Prince John" because of his fondness

"Attack of the rebels upon our gun-boat flotilla at Galveston, Texas, January 1, 1863." From *Harper's Weekly*, January 31, 1863. *CN 06262. Courtesy Prints and Photographs Collection, Center for American History, University of Texas at Austin.*

for elegant uniforms, fine food and drink, and the theater, was an experienced soldier with a reputation as a man of action. His presence in Texas concerned Renshaw, who wanted to withdraw from Galveston until he received reinforcements.

Renshaw was somewhat relieved when three companies of Massachusetts infantry, approximately 260 men, commanded by Col. Isaac S. Burrell arrived from New Orleans on Christmas Day. Renshaw was assured that the rest of the regiment, numbering seven hundred men, would arrive within a few days.[19]

Renshaw was correct in his belief that the Confederates intended to retake the island. The moment he arrived in Texas General Magruder began planning for an attack on the federals occupying Galveston. In December Magruder wrote and talked to Texas and Confederate authorities about little else. By the last week of the year he had assembled a force of several thousand men. These included the Twenty-sixth Texas Cavalry commanded by French military academy graduate Col. Xavier Blanchard Debray, the Twentieth Texas Infantry led by Col. Henry M. Elmore, units of the New Mexico Sibley Brigade led by Cols. Tom Green and Arthur P. Bagby, a battalion of the Second Texas Cavalry that had served under John R. Baylor in New Mexico and was commanded by Maj. Charles L. Pyron, several batteries from Col. Joseph J. Cook's First Texas Heavy Artillery, and assorted state militia units. In addition, Magruder acquired two steamboats, *Bayou City* and *Neptune*, which were converted into gunboats. *Bayou City*, a former river steamer, was armed with a thirty-two-pounder cannon; *Neptune*, a former mail packet, carried two twenty-four-pounder howitzers. Two smaller vessels, *John F. Carr* and *Lucy Gwinn*, served as tenders for Magruder's "fleet."[20]

Magruder planned to use his forces in a combined land and water attack. Under the cover of darkness the ground troops commanded by recently promoted Brig. Gen. William R. Scurry would cross over the abandoned railroad bridge that linked the island to the mainland. Then, after moving artilley into place, the Confederates would attack the Union troops barracked on Kuhn's Wharf. At the same time the Confederate flotilla, commanded by Commodore Leon Smith, an experienced steamboat captain whom Magruder had met in California years earlier, would descend from the upper part of Galveston Bay to attack the federal warships in the harbor. Tom Green and 150 men from the Fifth Texas would be on board *Bayou City*; A. P. Bagby and one hundred men of the Seventh Texas would be on *Neptune*. These cavalry veterans of the New Mexico campaign, protected only slightly by cotton bales on the decks of the vessels, would serve as sharpshooters until the Confederates came alongside the enemy. Then, acting as marines, the cavalrymen would board the enemy warships.[21]

In late December Magruder was ready to attack. Shortly after midnight on January 1, 1863, Magruder and Scurry led their troops from Virginia Point on the mainland across the railroad bridge to the island. Under cover of darkness they moved quietly into the center of town. At 4 A.M. Confederate artillery opened fire

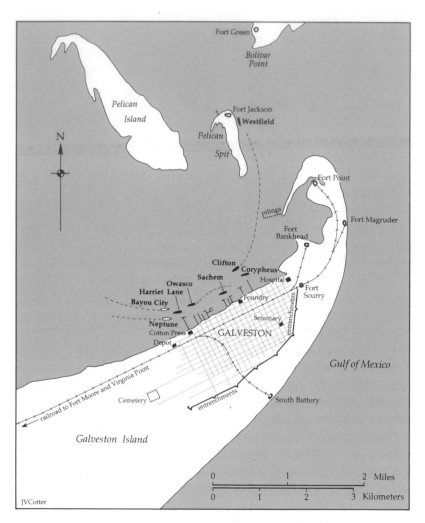

Battle of Galveston. *Map by John V. Cotter.*

upon Union positions along the waterfront. Colonel Cook then led five hundred men in an attempt to storm the Union positions on Kuhn's Wharf. Cook's troops advanced toward their objective but were forced to fall back under heavy enemy fire from Union troops on the wharf and the federal gunboats *Sachem*, *Owasco*, and

Corypheus. With Magruder's permission General Scurry began withdrawing his artillery to avoid the enemy fire.[22]

Just as the Confederate ground attack appeared to be failing, the Confederate gunboats *Bayou City* and *Neptune* steamed into the harbor. They moved toward the *Harriet Lane*, the most powerful of the Union ships, which was to the east of *Sachem*, *Owasco*, and *Corypheus*. As the ships began to exchange fire it appeared that the federals would be victorious. The *Harriet Lane* with five guns had greater firepower than the two Confederate vessels. The *Bayou City* was at the mercy of the enemy after

Texas Marine Department officers, left to right, Capt. Jno. Hall, Signal Officer G. A. Fosgard, 1st Engineer ———— Donehue, unknown Sailing Master, 2nd Engineer James Edwards, and Super Cargo Henry S. Lubbock. *From the SUGG Studio, Houston, ca. 1867 to 1870; courtesy the J. Dale West Collection, Longview.*

its thirty-two-pounder cannon exploded, killing several artillerymen. A few minutes later *Neptune* was hit by a shell from one of the *Lane*'s Dahlgren cannon and began sinking in shallow water.

The Confederates did not give up. Rifle fire from Green's sharpshooters on *Bayou City* and Bagby's men on the sinking *Neptune* forced seamen on the *Harriet Lane* below deck. The *Bayou City*, captained by Henry S. Lubbock, brother of the Texas governor, managed to ram the *Lane*, locking the two ships together. Commodore Smith, cutlass in hand, leaped to the deck of the *Lane* with Green's troopers following him. In the fighting that followed Capt. Jonathan M. Wainwright, Lt. Commander Edward Lea, and most of the officers of the *Lane* were killed. Surviving crewmen surrendered the ship.[23]

From that moment on, confusion prevailed in the Union naval command. The *Owasco*, a gunboat built for blockade service, steamed to the rescue of the *Harriet Lane*, but was was forced to pull away due to rifle fire from Green's men. Meanwhile, William B. Renshaw, commander of the Union flotilla, was having trouble of his own. During the darkness of the night his ship, *Westfield*, a converted New York ferryboat, ran aground on Pelican Spit near the mouth of the harbor. Efforts by a sister ship, *Clifton*, to move her were unsuccessful. The *Clifton* was then ordered to aid the smaller *Sachem* and *Corypheus* attempting to silence the Confederate shore batteries, but the federal efforts were poorly coordinated and ineffective.

Meanwhile, Commodore Smith and Captain Lubbock demanded the surrender of the other Union ships in the harbor. Commander Renshaw refused to consider the possibilities of surrender, but not knowing the size of the Confederate forces or the condition of the captured *Lane*, decided to scuttle the grounded *Westfield* and withdraw the rest of his ships from the harbor. He transferred most of his crew to the transport vessels *Saxon* and *Mary Boardman*, set fire to an improvised explosive charge on the *Westfield*, and was descending the ladder to a small boat when the charge prematurely blew up, killing him and the crew of the small boat. Lt. Commander Richard L. Law of the *Clifton*, the next ranking officer of the Union fleet, ordered the other federal vessels to withdraw from the harbor and head towards New Orleans. Commander Smith, boarding the tender *John F. Carr*, gave chase but the Union fleet soon outdistanced the *Carr*.

Colonel Burrell, commander of the Massachusetts troops on the waterfront, watched as the Union fleet sailed away. Believing that further resistance without gunboat support was futile, Burrell surrendered his 260 troops to Brigadier General Scurry. The battle of Galveston was over.[24]

While Texans rejoiced at the news of Galveston's liberation, Union authorities were angry. David G. Farragut, commanding the West Gulf Blockading Squadron, wanted to retake Galveston as soon as possible. In early January he ordered Commodore Henry Bell with another Union flotilla to recapture Galveston, but the appearance of the *C.S.S. Alabama* off the Texas coast thwarted federal efforts. One of Bell's gunboats, *Hatteras*, was sunk in an encounter with the Confederate raider. That same month Confederates at Sabine Pass, using two river steamers, the *Josiah H. Bell* and the *Uncle Ben*, captured two Union blockaders, the *Morning Light* and *Velocity*. This daring action and the loss of *Hatteras* convinced Bell that Confederates were stronger on the upper Texas coast than he had believed.[25]

There was no fighting along the Texas coast in the spring and summer of 1863. The Union Navy maintained its blockade but due to the campaigns in Louisiana and along the Mississippi lacked the resources to attempt any major operations in Texas waters. Meanwhile, General Magruder took steps to strengthen coastal defenses from Matagorda Bay to Sabine Pass. Guns from the wrecked warship *Westfield* and from the interior of the state were emplaced at Galveston. A new earthen and log fort was built with slave labor at Sabine Pass several hundred yards above old Fort Sabine. The new fortification was known locally as Fort Griffin, for

THEN AND NOW

With a population of slightly over six thousand inhabitants, Galveston was the second-largest city in Texas when the Civil War began. Sometimes referred to as "the New York of Texas," the isle city was the center of financial and commercial activity for the state. Today Galveston offers much to those interested in history. The Strand National Historic Landmark District, where the battle took place, has one of the nation's finest collections of restored Victorian architecture. The Strand Visitors Center, operated by the Galveston Historical Foundation, is located in the 1859 Hendley Building, the most important Civil War–era structure still remaining in the city. The building originally had a cupola, or observatory, on its roof, which provided an excellent view of the harbor and the Gulf of Mexico. During the Civil War the observatory was used by lookouts to spot Union blockaders.

In 1998 the Texas Historical Commission unveiled a state monument commemorating the battle of Galveston. The monument is located at the 1859 U.S. Customs House at 20th and Post Office Streets. A Galveston County Historical Commission marker is located at the Texas Seaport Museum on Pier 21 between 21st and 22nd Streets. The Galveston Wharves, a private facility, occupies the former site of Kuhn's Wharf at the foot of 18th Street.

Battle of Sabine Pass. Painting by A. J. Hamilton, ca. 1931. *CN 03502. Photograph courtesy Prints and Photographs Collection, Center for American History, University of Texas at Austin.*

Col. W. H. Griffin who commanded Confederates at Sabine Pass in the summer of 1863. Triangular in shape, the fort had a sawtooth front where six cannon were emplaced. Company F of the First Texas Heavy Artillery, known as the Davis Guard, garrisoned the fort. The Guard, a company of Irishmen from Houston command-ed by Capt. Frederick Odlum, had taken part in the battle of Galveston and the capture of the *Morning Light* and *Velocity*.[26]

In August 1863, Magruder received reports that Union general Nathaniel P. Banks was mounting a massive force for an invasion of Texas. Vicksburg and Port Hudson had been captured in July and President Lincoln now wanted to create a federal presence in Texas as a counterbalance to the French forces in Mexico.[27]

The federal attack came at Sabine Pass in early September. Sabine Pass was chosen because it was believed the area was weakly defended. Once captured it would allow access to Beau-mont, which historian Alwyn Barr points out was "a perfect base for operations in Texas because of its rail connection with Houston over flat country." Banks appointed William B. Franklin, a veteran campaigner with the Army of the Potomac in Virginia, as overall commander of the expedition. Five thousand troops of the Nine-teenth Army Corps commanded by Brig. Gen. Godfrey Weitzel

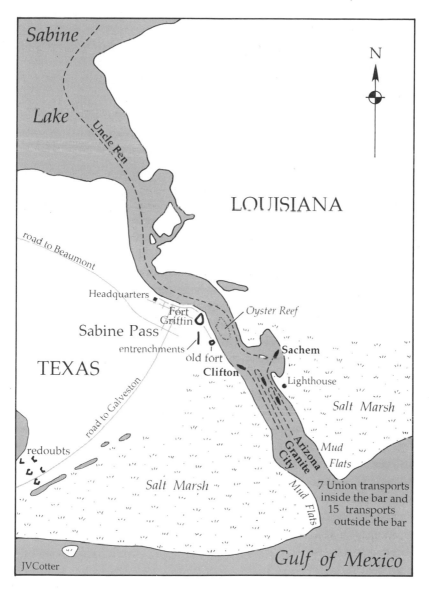

Sabine

Lake

Uncle Ren

LOUISIANA

road to Beaumont

Headquarters

Fort
Griffin

Sabine Pass

entrenchments

Oyster Reef

TEXAS

old fort

Sachem

Clifton

Lighthouse

road to Galveston

Salt Marsh

redoubts

Mud
Flats

Arizona
Granite
City

Salt Marsh

Mud Flats

7 Union transports
inside the bar and
15 transports
outside the bar

JVCotter

Gulf of Mexico

N

Battle of Sabine Pass. *Map by John V. Cotter.*

and a naval flotilla of twenty-two transport vessels and four light-draft gunboats commanded by navy lieutenant Frederick Crocker were assigned for the operation. The expedition left New Orleans on September 4 but did not reach the Sabine Pass area until midnight on September 6.[28]

Franklin originally planned to land his troops on the beaches west of Sabine Pass and attack Fort Griffin with Weitzel's infantry. He decided instead to have his gunboats enter the pass and shell the forts before the infantry landed. Early on the morning of September 8, the gunboat *Clifton*, one of the survivors of the battle of Galveston now commanded by Lieutenant Crocker, crossed the bar at the mouth of the pass and steamed into the channel. When within about fifteen hundred yards of the fort, *Clifton* opened fire. Twenty-six shells were fired but because of the range had little effect. Lt. Richard "Dick" Dowling, who was commanding Fort Griffin during the absence of Captain Odlum, kept his men under cover until the enemy was within closer range.[29]

Shortly after 7:00 A.M., the *Clifton* ceased firing. Crocker, impressed with the apparent strength of Fort Griffin, steamed back to the mouth of the pass, where he convinced Franklin to modify his plan again so that the Union infantry would come ashore while the gunboats fired on the fort. Meanwhile, the Confederates prepared to meet the attack. Captain Odlum, in temporary command of the post of Sabine Pass, alerted Beaumont and Houston of the Union threat and took steps to move ammunition to Fort Griffin. The *Uncle Ben*, a small Confederate gunboat on the Sabine, was dispatched to assist the Fort Griffin defenders. The *Uncle Ben* steamed down Sabine Lake to the upper end of the pass but was forced to pull back when the more powerful Union gunboat *Sachem* opened fire.

The Union attack began in the early afternoon. Union gunboats *Sachem* and *Arizona* came up the Louisiana side of the channel, while Crocker's *Clifton* moved up the Texas channel nearest to the fort. The *Granite City*, which came behind the *Clifton*, was to cover the landing of twelve hundred assault troops being carried by seven transport vessels. When the lead ships *Sachem* and *Clifton* came within twelve hundred yards of the fort, Dowling's gunners, who

THEN AND NOW

The battle of Sabine Pass took place just south of the town of Sabine Pass in the southeastern part of Jefferson County. The town, first known as the City of Sabine, was laid out in 1839 and projected to be a major Gulf seaport. The first steam sawmill in the county was built there in 1846. By the time of the Civil War the town had a post office, a newspaper, and a connection with the Eastern Texas Railroad. An outbreak of yellow fever in the summer of 1862 caused most residents to evacuate but many returned when the fever abated in the fall.

In 1936, Jefferson County purchased 1.65 acres of land which included the original site of Fort Griffin and established a park to commemorate the Confederate victory. An impressive monument to the Davis Guard, topped by a larger-than-life-sized bronze statue of Lt. Richard W. "Dick" Dowling created by sculptor Herring Coe, was dedicated on May 22, 1937.

In 1971, the Texas Parks and Wildlife Department purchased additional land (over fifty acres) and established the Sabine Pass Battleground State Historical Park. A series of historical markers in the park note the site of Fort Griffin, United States forces at Sabine Pass, United States dead at the battle of Sabine Pass (federal sailors and soldiers killed were interred near this site), Spaight's Eleventh Battalion (the local volunteers who defended the Texas and Louisiana coasts during the war), Fort Manhassett (built 7.5 miles west in October 1863), and Kate Dorman (a resident of Sabine Pass who aided Confederate troops stationed at Fort Griffin).

An open-air pavilion provides several information panels describing the battle. There are no original fortifications still existing. Also located in the park are four concrete ammunition bunkers which were built for the use of a coastal artillery battery protecting the entrance of Sabine Pass during the Second World War.

Some artifacts from the battle of Sabine Pass may be viewed at the Museum of the Gulf Coast, 700 Procter Street, in Port Arthur.

had daily practiced sighting their weapons at that range, opened a murderous fire. A shell from one of the fort's twenty-four-pounders ripped through the steam drum of *Sachem*, throwing scalding steam and water on the crew. Additional hits from the Confederate guns left *Sachem* a helpless wreck, with bodies of the dead and wounded piled high.[30]

Dowling's gunners now turned their attention to the *Clifton*. A

THEN AND NOW

Indianola, which was occupied by federal troops during the winter of 1863–64, was the chief port through which many European immigrants had come into Texas. Founded as Indian Point in 1846, the town grew rapidly in the decade before the Civil War and became the second-busiest port in Texas. Its growth continued after the war. It had a population of five thousand when a devastating hurricane destroyed much of the town in September 1875. After being partially rebuilt the town was almost obliterated by a second hurricane in August 1886. By 1887 the orginal town had been abandoned. A small settlement with the same name exists nearby today.

A Texas historical marker at the end of State Highway 316 provides a brief history of the town and Fort Esperanza which controlled the gateway to Indianola through Pass Cavallo.

Confederate shot hit the *Clifton*'s tiller rope, throwing her out of control and into the mud. Crocker, a gallant and determined officer, continued to fight until the ship's boiler exploded from a direct hit. Someone on the *Clifton* struck her flag to surrender. Many of her crew, thinking the ship was about to explode, jumped overboard and struggled to reach shore where they surrendered to Dowling and his men.

The *Arizona, Granite City,* and the transport vessels withdrew from the pass, leaving *Sachem, Clifton,* and their crews in Confederate hands. General Franklin, convinced that the Confederates were much stronger than they actually were, ordered the withdrawal of his fleet to New Orleans.[31]

The battle at Sabine Pass lasted less than an hour. In that time Dowling and the forty-two men under his command captured two gunboats, captured or killed 350 of the enemy, and caused the Union task force of over twenty ships and five thousand men to leave the scene. Although several of the Confederates, including Dowling, received powder burns there were no casualties among the defenders. General Magruder praised Dowling and his men "as the greatest heroes that history has recorded." President Davis described the defense of Sabine Pass as "one of the most brilliant and heroic achievements in the history of this war." A special

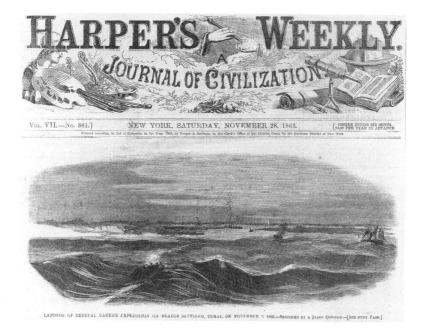

HARPER'S WEEKLY.

JOURNAL OF CIVILIZATION.

VOL. VII.—No. 361.] NEW YORK, SATURDAY, NOVEMBER 28, 1863. [SINGLE COPIES SIX CENTS.
[$3.00 PER YEAR IN ADVANCE.]

Entered according to Act of Congress, in the Year 1863, by Harper & Brothers, in the Clerk's Office of the District Court for the Southern District of New York.

LANDING OF GENERAL BANKS'S EXPEDITION ON BRAZOS SANTIAGO, TEXAS, ON NOVEMBER 2, 1863.—SKETCHED BY A STAFF OFFICER.—[SEE NEXT PAGE.]

"Landing of General Banks's Expedition on Brazos Santiago, Texas," November 2, 1863. From *Harper's Weekly*, November 28, 1863. *Photograph courtesy Jerry Thompson, Laredo.*

medal, suspended from a green ribbon, was struck for each member of the Davis Guard. One of the medals was sent to President Davis who carried it on his person until he was taken prisoner in May 1865.[32]

Although elated with the victory at Sabine Pass, Magruder believed the enemy would make other efforts to penetrate southeast Texas. Accordingly, he moved the Third Texas Infantry, the Twentieth Texas Infantry, and the Twenty-third Texas Cavalry, and several artillery batteries to Sabine Pass. Long-range Parrot rifles from the captured *Sachem* replaced some of the smoothbore pieces at Fort Griffin. In addition, Magruder pushed the completion of a new fort, Manhassett, west of Sabine Pass, to prevent a possible enemy flanking movement from the rear of Fort Griffin.[33]

General Banks, the federal commander in New Orleans, had no intention of repeating the attack on Sabine Pass. But still under pressure from the Lincoln administration, Banks decided to move against South Texas. On November 2, 1863, Banks and an army of seven thousand troops, transported by twenty-six ships, landed at Brazos Santiago, near the mouth of the Rio Grande. Confederate Brig. Gen. Hamilton P. Bee, commanding the Rio Grande subdistrict, had fewer than one hundred men with which to defend Brownsville. Bee decided to evacuate the city after loading forty-five wagons with supplies that were taken into the interior. As he left, Bee set fire to cotton and stores that could not be moved. On November 6, Union troops occupied Brownsville.[34]

After the capture of Brownsville, Union troops moved against various points along the lower and middle Texas coast. In late November they occupied Mustang, St. Joseph, and Matagorda Islands. Fort Esperanza on the northeastern tip of Matagorda Island, garrisoned by five hundred men with eight heavy cannons, was abandoned by the Confederates on November 29 after the guns were spiked and magazines set on fire. In December Union troops occupied Indianola and Port Lavaca on the mainland. At the same time two regiments of Texans serving in the Union Army commanded by Col. Edmund J. Davis and Col. John L. Haynes moved up the Rio Grande to occupy Ringgold Barracks near Rio Grande City.[35]

General Magruder believed there was little he could do to prevent Union control of South Texas. He was convinced that the next federal move would be in the region of the lower Brazos River. As 1863 ended he began concentrating all available troops to meet an expected invasion there.

Confederate soldier and sweetheart, Henderson County, Texas. *Courtesy Lawrence T. Jones III, Austin.*

3.
LIVING IN CONFEDERATE TEXAS

BY THE END OF 1863 the vast majority of adult white male Texans, ninety thousand according to Gov. Francis Lubbock, were serving in Confederate or state military forces, some far away from the state. Those men, women, and children who remained at home faced new challenges as they adjusted to the impact of war.

A frontier state, Texas suffered less than the other Confederate states. The major battles of the war were fought in Virginia, Tennessee, and Georgia, where physical devastation was immense. Although Galveston was occupied briefly, Brownsville, Indianola, and South Texas were under federal control in the winter of 1863–64, and El Paso was occupied by federal troops following Sibley's retreat in 1862, most of those living in Texas did not have direct contact with the enemy. Even so, there were changes in lifestyles. The blockade of the Southern coastline cut off many imports from Europe and other parts of the world. Too, the great variety of goods purchased from Northern manufacturers were no longer available. As a result, there were shortages of many items, especially coffee, medicine, clothing, shoes, and farm implements.

Some Texans were using substitutes to replace imported coffee as early as the fall of 1861. A Confederate soldier, David Kennard, stationed at Virginia Point across from Galveston Island, wrote to his parents on November 28, 1861, explaining that he had learned how to make potato coffee. Young Kennard apparently found the substitute fairly satisfactory. Not everyone was so agreeable. The British visitor Lt. Col. Arthur Fremantle noted that "the loss of coffee affects the Confederates even more than their loss of spirits; and they exercise their ingenuity in devising substitutes, most of which are not generally very successful." While traveling through East Texas, Fremantle was served a mixture called Confederate coffee, made of rye, meal, Indian corn, and sweet potatoes. Eliza McHatton Ripley, a refugee from Louisiana in Texas, observed that peanuts, sweet potatoes, rye, beans, peas, and cornmeal were used as coffee substitutes, all of which she called "wretched imitations, though gulped down, when chilly and tired, for lack of anything better."[36]

In her travels in Texas, Mrs. McHatton-Ripley noted that "all household and family goods were scarce." "A needle dropped or mislaid was searched after for hours; if one was broken its irreparable loss was lamented," she observed. Amelia Barr, the Englishwoman who later became one of America's most prolific authors, lived in Austin with her family during the war. In her memoirs she recalled that because of the shortage of pins and needles "some were compelled to use mesquite thorns for pins."[37]

Some newspapers suspended publication because of the shortage of paper, while others reduced their issues to smaller size. Shortages of salt occurred after federal armies overran Saltville, Virginia, and Avery Island, Louisiana, two major sources of commercial salt for the Confederacy. Salt became so scarce that some Texans dug up the floors of smokehouses and leached the dirt to recover the salt drippings. Bark, herbs, and berries were used for dyes, willow bark and red pepper were mixed as a substitute for quinine, and backs of wallpaper served as writing paper. Occasionally there were shortages of specific food items, but apparently these were not so serious as those leading to bread riots in Richmond, Mobile, and Atlanta.[38]

The shortage of commodities was exasperated by the large number of refugees who came to Texas from Arkansas and Louisiana to escape invading Union armies. East Texas, especially the towns of Tyler, Rusk, Marshall, and Corsicana, was particularly affected by this onrush of refugees. The city of Houston also received refugees from Galveston as a result of that city's federal occupation. Many of the refugees found life in Texas to be harsh. They complained of heat, dust, wind, insects, reptiles, and boorish neighbors. Young Kate Stone of Brokenburn plantation in northern Louisiana believed she had discovered "the dark corner of the Confederacy" in East Texas. Most refugees adjusted to conditions in the Lone Star State, however. Even Stone, who complained constantly about poor accommodations and unsanitary conditions, later admitted that the last twelve months she spent in Confederate Texas "was the happiest year" of her life.[39]

Trade through Mexico allowed Texans to obtain some of the goods that in normal times came through Gulf ports. In exchange for cotton, Texans received military supplies, medicines, dry goods, ironware, liquors, and coffee. By the end of the first year of the war, wagon trains moved across South Texas carrying thousands of bales of cotton from Texas, Arkansas, and Louisiana plantations and farms. Almost overnight Matamoros, the Mexican town across the Rio Grande from Brownsville, became a thriving metropolis with cotton buyers, speculators, agents, and merchants from all over the world eager to obtain cotton. From Matamoros cotton was taken in river steamers down the Rio Grande to Bagdad, a small town on the coast, for transshipment to oceangoing vessels. By the time of the Union occupation of Brownsville more than 150,000 bales of cotton had passed through Matamoros. When Brownsville was captured, the Texans moved the trade upriver to Laredo and then down the Mexican side of the Rio Grande. By the end of the war 320,000 bales of cotton had been shipped across the Rio Grande.[40]

Some goods continued to be brought into Texas through the Union naval blockade by fast steamers or sailing schooners. Galveston was the favorite port for blockade runners but Sabine Pass, Velasco, Matagorda, Indianola, and Corpus Christi were ports of call for those bold enough to run the blockade. Most of the Texas trade went through Havana, Cuba. Fast, light vessels made the dash across the Gulf. Once in Cuba, cotton was transferred to larger, neutral flagships heading for Europe, or in some cases a seaport in the United States. Returning vessels brought war materials or consumer goods to Havana; these were then transferred to blockade runners heading for Texas. The exact number of such attempts is unknown but most historians believe blockade runners came in and out of Texas ports well over a thousand times. The majority of these runs were successful. Historian Tuffly Ellis estimates blockade runners were captured in only 10 to 15 percent of their voyages in and out of Texas ports.[41]

Control of the cotton trade became an issue of dispute between Edmund Kirby Smith, the Confederate commander of the Trans-Mississippi Department, and Pendleton Murrah, who succeeded Francis Lubbock as governor in 1863. Smith created a Cotton Bureau through which his department attempted to purchase and resell Texas cotton, the profits of which would be used for purchasing military supplies. Texas planters protested what they considered to be unfair costs for transporting their cotton to bureau depots. Too, they resented the threat of impressment if they did not cooperate with the bureau. Under Governor Murrah's leadership, the Texas legislature created its own cotton plan, which gave Texas planters protection from Confederate impressment. General Smith complained that the Texas plan hurt his efforts to provide arms and ammunition for his troops. For a brief time an impasse prevailed, but Murrah finally agreed to appeal to Texas planters to deliver their cotton to Smith's bureau for sale.[42]

A more serious disagreement between Confederate authorities and Texas officials occurred over conscription. State leaders argued that individuals enrolled in the militia were not subject to Confederate conscription laws, a position with which General Magruder and Elkanah Greer, head of the Conscript Bureau of the Trans-Mississippi Department, strongly disagreed. The issue came to a head with the passage of two new militia acts by the Texas legislature in December 1863. One measure, which created what came to be called the Frontier Organization, declared that adult white males residing in frontier counties were to be organized into militia companies for border defense. Another act provided that able-bodied men living elsewhere in Texas would be retained in the state militia. Generals Smith and Magruder argued that these laws conflicted with Confederate laws which had superiority over state statutes. After some quarreling between officials, Murrah agreed to a compromise whereby the state would retain militiamen already under arms but these men would be subject to Confederate authority in an emergency. On the issue of conscripts who resided in frontier counties, however, Murrah refused to budge. He insisted that these individuals serve in the Frontier Organization. The matter was referred to Richmond for resolution, but the war ended before the matter was resolved.[43]

Although Murrah disagreed with Confederate officials over matters such as conscription, impressment, and the cotton trade, Texas leaders generally were cooperative with both Kirby Smith and Richmond authorities. Murrah's predecessors as governor, Edward Clark and Francis Lubbock, worked closely with Confederate officials in recruiting, organizing, and equipping military units from Texas for Confederate service. Clark, who became governor when Houston refused to take the Confederate oath of loyalty, served as chief executive for less than a year. Lubbock, who narrowly defeated Clark in the autumn elections of 1861, was a staunch supporter of the Davis administration and worked tirelessly to improve state-national relations. In the summer of 1862 he issued an invitation to the governors of Arkansas, Missouri, and Louisiana to meet with him at Marshall, Texas, to discuss issues of mutual concern to the Trans-Mississippi states. A second conference was held at Marshall in August 1863, this time at the request of departmental commander Kirby Smith. Lubbock believed that both conferences led to improved relations and greater cooperation between state and Confederate officials.[44]

Lubbock and Murrah had to deal with those Texans who remained loyal to the Union and did not support the Confederacy. Some Texans opposed secession and the Confederacy at the outset but later came to accept the Confederacy. James W. Throckmorton of Collin County was perhaps the best known of this group. Throckmorton, leader of the eight delegates in the Secession Convention who voted against disunion, served as a regimental commander in the Confederate Army and was later a brigadier general in state service. Ben H. Epperson, a lawyer and businessman from Red River County, was a Unionist who urged Sam

THEN AND NOW

Marshall, Texas, was the location of three conferences of Trans-Mississippi governors during the Civil War. In addition to the 1862 and 1863 meetings described in the text, a third meeting was held in Marshall in May 1865, to discuss surrender terms proposed by Union general John Pope.

Marshall is the seat of Harrison County, one of the richest cotton producing counties in antebellum Texas. Harrison County (6,217 free inhabitants and 8,784 slaves) had the third largest population in Texas on the eve of the Civil War. The town of Marshall had a population of nearly three thousand people. During the war numerous manufacturing, governmental, and military offices were located in Marshall. The Confederate governor and other officials of Missouri made Marshall their capital after Union occupation of the state. The homes at the corner of Bolivar and Crockett Streets used as the executive mansion and capitol building for Missouri governor Thomas C. Reynolds and his staff were both razed in 1950 and replaced by modern buildings.

The Harrison County Historical Museum, located in the old courthouse in the center of town, has artifacts and displays relating to the Civil War. Historical markers on US 58 and US 80 describe the city's role in the Civil War. A Confederate monument created by noted sculptor Frank Teich at the old courthouse commemorates the thirteen Confederate companies sworn into service near the site. The city has a number of lovely nineteenth-century homes, but most were built after the war. Several antebellum-Civil War era homes are located in the area. These include Mimosa Hall, home of John J. Webster, Freeman Plantation, one mile west of Jefferson on State Highway 49, Sagamore, at the corner of Dixon and Owen streets in Jefferson, and the Alley-McKay House, 306 Delta Street in Jefferson. Most are open at certain hours for public tours.

Houston to resist secession, but once the war was underway contributed money to raise and equip Confederate troops. Galveston lawyer William Pitt Ballinger opposed secession but helped to acquire artillery for the defense of the island and was later appointed receiver of confiscated enemy property. Wealthy slaveholder and Unionist William C. Young of Cooke County raised a regiment of Confederate cavalry, which he led in occupying federal posts in Indian Territory.[45]

The majority of Texas Unionists did not become supporters of the Confederacy like Throckmorton, Epperson, Ballinger, and

36

Young. Some, like Elisha M. Pease and David G. Burnet, attempted to be neutral or to remain silent while the war went on. Others found neutrality or silence more difficult. Attorney George W. Paschal, a friend and associate of former governors Pease and Houston, tried to accept the decision of his fellow Texans regarding secession, but spoke out against conscription, impressment, and other measures he considered unconstitutional, leading to his arrest and imprisonment by local authorities. Similarly, Texas Unionists George Whitmore, an East Texas state representative, and Dr. Richard Peebles, one of the founders of Hempstead, were arrested for their opposition to the Confederacy.[46]

Sam Houston accepted the will of the people on the issue of secession but continued to criticize actions of the government he believed to be illegal or undemocratic. When his oldest son, Sam Houston Jr., joined the Bayland Guards of the Second Texas Infantry, the old hero of San Jacinto often visited the drills and claimed to be a private in the company. Houston followed the news of the war closely, criticizing fellow Texan Albert Sidney Johnston (who had been an ally of Houston's old rival Mirabeau B. Lamar) for his failures in Kentucky and Tennessee and congratulating John B. Magruder for "driving from our soil a ruthless enemy." Houston remained a critic of Confederate President Jefferson Davis, with whom he had served in the United States Senate. In one of his last letters written before his death in July 1863, Houston declared that Davis "deserves to be shot" for the appointment of incompetent generals like Henry H. Sibley.[47]

Some Texas Unionists fled from the state to avoid conflict. James P. Newcomb, editor of the *Alamo Express*, left for Mexico after a mob wrecked his office. Noah Smithwick, pioneer blacksmith and veteran of the Texas Revolution, went to California where he lived for the next thirty-eight years. Unionist Swen Magnus Swenson, Swedish merchant, banker, planter, and rancher, remained in Texas for two years after secession, but fled the state in fear for his life in the autumn of 1863. He spent the rest of the war in Mexico and New Orleans. A close friend, federal judge Thomas DuVal of Austin, also lived the latter part of the war in New Orleans. Melinda Rankin, Northern-born missionary and teacher, was another

Sam Houston, engraving by W. J. Edwards, after daguerreotype by Mathew B. Brady. *CN 0095a. Courtesy Prints and Photographs Collection, Center for American History, University of Texas at Austin.*

Unionist who left the state. She returned to Brownsville during the federal occupation but departed when the Union Army pulled out. Wealthy merchant, cotton broker, and railroad developer William Marsh Rice transferred his business to Matamoros, where he continued his business ventures. He moved to New York City after the war but retained commercial interests in Texas.[48]

Slightly over two thousand Texans, including forty-seven African Americans and 958 Mexican Americans, served in the Union Army. Edmund Jackson Davis, a native of Florida who had lived in Texas since 1848, became leader of this group. A successful attorney and judge in South Texas, Davis opposed secession but declared he accepted the decision of the people on this issue. Like Sam Houston, however, Davis refused to take the oath of allegiance to the Confederacy. After a year of controversy with local Confederates he left for Mexico. From there he journeyed to Washington, where he received a colonel's commission and authorization to raise a regiment of cavalry. He returned to New Orleans, where he recruited Texans who had left their home rather than serve the Confederacy. His regiment, the First Texas Cavalry (Union), served briefly in campaigns in the Louisiana bayou country in 1863 and came to Texas with the Union Army that occupied Brownsville in November 1863.[49]

John L. Haynes, veteran of the Mexican War and state representative from Starr County, followed Edmund J. Davis to Mexico in March 1862. A native of Virginia, Haynes had lived in South Texas for over a decade. During that time he prospered as a merchant and married Angelica Wells, a granddaughter of Martin Van Buren. He was very sympathetic to Mexican Texans and rejected the strong anti-Tejano attitude of Anglo leaders. He traveled with Davis to New Orleans and Washington and helped organize the First Texas Cavalry (Union). When a second regiment of Unionist cavalry was formed at Brownsville in December 1863, Haynes became its commander. Over half of the recruits of Haynes's regiment were Mexican Americans, the majority born in Mexico. Many of these Tejanos and Mexicanos joined the Union Army as a means to strike back at their old oppressors in Confederate Texas. In the spring of 1864 the First and Second Texas Cavalry (Union) formed a cavalry brigade, commanded by Davis, who was later promoted to the rank of brigadier general.[50]

Andrew Jackson Hamilton was another Texan who became a brigadier general in Union service. An Austin lawyer, state representative, and political ally of Sam Houston, Jack Hamilton was elected to the United States Congress as an Independent Democrat in 1858. He opposed secession and worked with Southern and Northern moderates who attempted unsuccessfully to find a compromise to the sectional controversy. In the spring of 1862 he and several fellow Unionists fled to Mexico. From there he traveled to Washington, where he met with President Lincoln. Hamilton was appointed brigadier general of volunteers and military governor of Texas. Along with Edmund J. Davis he returned to Texas with Banks's army in late 1863. When the Union Army withdrew from South Texas in 1864 Hamilton went to New Orleans, where he remained until the war ended.[51]

The extent of Unionist feeling in Texas is difficult to measure. The historian Claude Elliott estimated that one-third of the Texas population actively or passively supported the federal cause. He believed that another third of Texans remained neutral and only one-third actively supported the Confederacy. Elliott's estimate of Unionist strength is reasonable, but he probably understated the degree of support for the Confederacy in his calculations.[52]

Unionist support within the state was strongest in the German counties of Central Texas and in the North Texas counties along the Red River. While many German voters supported secession, others opposed disunion and resisted serving in the Confederate Army. In the Texas hill country, Germans organized a Union Loyal League, ostensibly to provide frontier protection. Confederate authorities considered the League subversive. In April 1862, Gen. Hamilton P. Bee, then commanding the Texas western subdistrict, declared martial law, a measure later extended to the entire state by Gen. Paul O. Hébert. Confederate officials sent Capt. James Duff and a detachment of Texas Partisan Rangers into the Fredericksburg area to enforce Confederate conscription laws and to disband military companies organized by the Union League.[53]

Most of the Unionist military companies were disbanded, but

Andrew Jackson Hamilton. *Courtesy Lawrence T. Jones III, Austin.*

FUNERAL OF GERMAN PATRIOTS AT COMFORT, TEXAS, August 20, 1865.—[See Page 39.]

"Funeral of German Patriots at Comfort, Texas." After the war, the bones of the dead Unionists massacred on the Nueces were gathered by E. Degener, father of two of the dead, along with other relatives and friends of the victims, and buried at Comfort on August 20, 1865. From *Harper's Weekly*, January 20, 1866. *Photograph courtesy Jerry Thompson, Laredo.*

sixty-one men led by Fritz Tegener attempted to leave the state and join the Union Army. They left the Kerrville area in early August heading for the Rio Grande. They were overtaken near the Nueces River on August 10 by a detachment of Partisan Rangers commanded by Lt. C. D. McRae. The larger and better equipped Ranger force made a surprise attack on the Unionists early that morning, killing thirty Germans and wounding eighteen others. The wounded Unionists were later executed by the Confederates. In his report of the so-called battle of the Nueces, McRae defended this action, writing that the Unionists "offered the most determined resistance and fought with desperation, asking no quarter whatever; hence, I have no prisoners to report . . ."[54]

Unionist sentiment was also prevalent in several northeast Texas counties. Some of the Unionists in the region formed a secret Peace Party opposed to military conscription and supportive of the Union. Local authorities were convinced that these dissenters were planning some type of insurrection. In October 1862, mass arrests of suspected Unionists occurred in Gainesville, the seat of Cooke County and suspected center of insurrectionist activity. A citizens' jury convicted and executed forty-two of those arrested in what came to be called "the great Gainesville hanging." In the next several weeks other suspected Unionists were hanged in neighboring Grayson, Wise, and Denton Counties.[55]

As the war continued, the number of those Texans avoiding military service grew. Some of these were dedicated Unionists opposed to the Confederacy; others were individuals who had served in the army but deserted for personal reasons. In the course of the war over four thousand Texans were listed as deserters. Nearly three-fourths of these lived in the woods and brush country of the northern subdistrict of Texas. Brig. Gen. Henry E. McCulloch, commander of the district, attempted to convince them to come in and give themselves up, but with little success. He eventually turned to Col. James Bourland, commander of the Border

THEN AND NOW

The battle of the Nueces took place at a bend in the west fork of the Nueces River in Kinney County. The battle site is located on private property and can be visited only by special arrangement with the owner. The museum at Fort Clark Springs in Brackettville provides some information on the battle.

The remains of the Unionists killed on the Nueces were later buried in Comfort, Texas, where many of those slain had resided. A monument with the inscription "*Treue Der Union*" (Loyalty to the Union) was erected on High Street (two blocks off State Highway 27) in 1866. The aging monument was restored in 1994 by master stonemason Karl H. Kuhn.

A Texas historical marker on Interstate Highway 35 in Gainesville provides information on the "great hanging" of 1862. Two other markers on State Highway 51 at the Elm Creek Bridge describe Cooke County support for the Confederacy and the Second Frontier Regiment headquartered at Gainesville. A life-sized granite statue of a Confederate soldier created by the McNeil Marble Company is located on the courthouse grounds. A marble Confederate soldier by sculptor Frank Teich is in Leonard Park, 1000 West California, Gainesville.

Sarah Devereux. Reproduction from original daguerreotype made in the early to mid-1850s, probably at Wirt's Photography, Pecan Street, Austin, Texas. *Photograph courtesy Marce Lowry Welch.*

Regiment, a tough-minded, disciplinarian known as the "Hangman of Texas," for assistance. Bourland was thorough but oftentimes ruthless in his pursuit of deserters. Stories circulated throughout the region that Bourland and his men frequently murdered suspected Unionists and deserters while holding them as prisoners.[56]

Although there was opposition to the war, the majority of white Texans supported the Confederacy and the war effort. Estimates of the number of Texans serving in the military vary, but it appears that four out of every five white adult males of military age were in Confederate or state military units at one time or another. This left a major responsibility for managing homes, farms, and plantations to the women. For some, such as Sarah Devereux of Rusk County and Rebecca Hagerty of Harrison County, this was not a new experience as they had supervised plantations before the war. For others, such as Lizzie Neblett of Grimes County and Mary America Connor of Cass County, this was a new undertaking, as they took over responsibilities for husbands in the army.[57]

Some Texas women entered professions, such as teaching, formerly reserved for men. Many performed volunteer work in hospitals and sick wards, formed aid societies to make sheets, pillowcases, and bandages, or assisted servicemen and their families to find food, clothing, and shelter. A few women served in the army disguised as men. Some, such as Sophia Butts Porter of Grayson County, provided Confederate authorities with information concerning enemy troop movements. Sally Scull, a legendary figure in South Texas, freighted cotton in wagons to the Rio

Grande, where she exchanged the cotton for guns and ammunition for the Confederacy. Kate Dorman and Sarah Vosburg of Sabine Pass brought food and drink to Dick Dowling and his men at Fort Griffin during the Union attack.[58]

Many Texas women who managed farms and plantations during the war had the responsibility of directing the work of African-American slaves. Texas had a slave population of 182,000 in 1860. This was increased by more than thirty thousand slaves "refugeed" by Arkansas, Louisiana, and Mississippi planters fleeing from federal forces that occupied these states. Although Confederate conscription laws exempted individuals supervising twenty or more slaves, few Texas planters took advantage of the law to escape military service, thus plantations and farms were operated by Texas women and older men during the war.

Most Texas slaves continued to labor as faithfully as before the war and caused little trouble for those supervising them. Historian Randolph Campbell points out that "slaves in Texas generally knew what the war meant, but they did relatively little to hinder the Confederate military effort or contribute to Union victory." No major slave rebellions occurred during the war and the number of those running away did not increase dramatically. This was due in part to a sense of loyalty some slaves felt toward white families and in part because there was little opportunity to do otherwise. When emancipation did come at the end of the war Texas slaves greeted the event with joy.[59]

Private John P. Offield, Company A, Twelfth Texas Cavalry (Parson's Brigade). *Courtesy Lawrence T. Jones III, Austin.*

4.
DEFENDING HOME AND COUNTRY

WHILE THE STRUGGLE to defend the Confederacy continued in 1863 and 1864, people in the northwestern counties of Texas fought to protect their homes from Indian attacks.

Just before Christmas 1863, a band of over three hundred Comanche Indians crossed the Red River and made a major raid into Montague and Cooke Counties, killing a dozen citizens, burning ten homes, and carrying off numerous horses and several women. Confederate and state troops gave pursuit but the raiders escaped back into Indian Territory before they could be overtaken.[60]

Although there were several small raids during the spring and summer of 1864, there was not another major Indian incursion until October 1864, when over five hundred Kiowas and Comanches led by the Comanche Little Buffalo crossed the Red River and rode southward into Young County. The raiders divided into several parties which attacked ranches and farms along Elm Creek, a tributary of the Brazos. Troops from Col. James Bourland's Frontier Regiment and Maj. William Quayle's Frontier District rode to assist families who took refuge in two small fortified stockades, but arrived after the Indians had withdrawn, taking seven women and children captives with them. The troopers followed the Indians for over one hundred miles before they gave up the chase.[61]

Confederate and state authorities were determined there would be no repetition of the Elm Creek raid. The practice of "forting

THEN AND NOW

Several Texas historical markers indicate the sites of various Indian raids and battles in Civil War Texas. The raid on Elm Creek in October 1864, is described on a marker located nine miles west of Newcastle in Young County off State Highway 24. Markers on the grounds of Fort Belknap, three miles south of State Highway 251 note that the Confederate frontier post of Camp Belknap was located nearby and that Tonkawa Indians served as scouts for Texas troops during the Civil War.

Historical markers 8.5 miles southwest of Mertzon near the Irion County line describe Texas Civil War Indian troubles and the January 8, 1865, battle of Dove Creek. The Dove Creek battle site, about twenty miles southwest of San Angelo, is on private property not open to the public.

A marker in Fort Griffin State Park, off US 283, at Albany names and describes various forts built as part of "forting up" by families against Indian attacks.

The battle site of Adobe Walls is on private land in Hutchinson County, approximately eighteen miles northeast of Stinett, Texas. A Texas historical marker at State Highway 15 and Farm Road 278, five miles north of Stinett, describes the battle.

up," or drawing settlers and livestock into fortified stockades or ranch houses, was continued and patrols were increased in an effort to provide more timely warnings of impending attacks. Fear of attacks led to an unfortunate clash with a band of migratory Kickapoos crossing Texas on their way to Mexico, apparently with only peaceful intentions. They were spotted by Texas scouts, and trailed by Confederate troops and state militia who overtook the Indians at Dove Creek, a tributary of the Concho, on January 8, 1865. In the battle that followed, the Kickapoos drove off the Texas attackers and continued on their way. Over forty Texans were killed or wounded in this unnecessary encounter; Indian losses were less than twenty.[62]

The only other major engagement with Indians in Civil War Texas was between Union troops and the Comanches and Kiowas. In November 1864, Col. Christopher "Kit" Carson, the famous frontiersman, led several hundred New Mexico Volunteers and Ute and Apache scouts into the Texas Panhandle in an effort to stop Indian attacks on wagon trains along the Santa Fe Trail. After destroying a large Kiowa village, Carson was overtaken by the Indians near the ruins of Fort Adobe, just north of the Canadian River. Using the old walls of the fort for protection, Carson and his troops withstood a series of attacks by a thousand Indians before withdrawing from what came to be known as the first battle of Adobe Walls.[63]

While West Texans were defending their homes from hostile Indian raids, the old Ranger captain John S. Ford was attempting to clear South Texas of federal troops. Ford, one of the most highly regarded Texans of his time, had been serving as superintendent of conscripts for Texas, a thankless task which he did not enjoy. He was pleased when General Magruder, Confederate commander of Texas, ordered him to form an expeditionary force to drive the federals from the lower Rio Grande valley.

After recruiting troops for what he called "the Cavalry of the West," Ford left San Antonio in mid-March 1864, heading for the Rio Grande. While en route he learned that two hundred federal troops commanded by Maj. Alfred E. Holt had attempted to seize Laredo but had been driven off by Col. Santos Benavides and a handful of Confederate Texans. Ford himself reached Laredo on April 15. He then moved down the river to occupy Ringgold Barracks near Rio Grande City. After a delay of several weeks caused by supply problems, Ford resumed his march southward. In late June the Confederates defeated several companies of the First Texas Union Cavalry at the village of Las Rucias.[64]

Ford, who had eighteen hundred men under his command, approached Brownsville cautiously, as the federal forces occupying the city were several times larger than his. In July he heard reports that the Union commander Maj. Gen. Francis J. Herron had withdrawn most of his troops from Texas to assist Maj. Gen. Nathaniel P. Banks in Louisiana. A small federal force was left behind to hold Brazos Island near the mouth of the Rio Grande. On July 30, 1864, one of Ford's patrols rode into Brownsville to find the federals had evacuated two days earlier.[65]

Ford moved quickly to occupy Brownsville and reestablish Confederate authority. Some unrest along the border continued for

ELIZABETH STREET, BROWNSVILLE, TEXAS.—[FROM A PHOTOGRAPH.]

"Elizabeth Street, Brownsville, Texas." On November 6, 1863, the Federals occupied Brownsville. From *Harper's Weekly*, December 16, 1865. *Photograph courtesy Jerry Thompson, Laredo.*

several months. Juan Cortina, who had fought against Ford and the Texans in the late 1850s, was now a general in the Mexican Army and military governor of Tamaulipas, the Mexican state across from Brownsville. Cortina, anxious to even the score with his old foes in Texas, suspended the cotton trade and in September 1864, opened artillery fire on the Confederates. At the same time federals on Brazos Island made an attack on Confederate outposts east of Brownsville, but were driven back. Conditions improved in late autumn when Mexican Imperialist and French forces drove Cortina from Matamoros. Ford established cordial relations with Gen. Tomas Mejia, the Imperialist commander, and the cotton trade was reopened. Relative calm prevailed in South Texas for the next several months.[66]

While John S. Ford and his cavalry were moving into South Texas, thousands of other Texans were fighting in northern Louisiana to keep Nathaniel P. Banks's Union army from advancing into East Texas. Banks, commander of Union forces in New

Orleans, launched a move up the Red River in early March. Banks planned to capture Shreveport and then turn toward the Marshall-Jefferson area, the location of numerous military warehouses, shops, factories, and administrative offices. Too, thousands of bales of cotton were stored in the region. Their capture would satisfy the needs of New England mill owners and deprive the Confederates of a commodity used in the foreign weapons trade.[67]

With naval support from Rear Admiral David Porter's fleet of gunboats and transports, Banks's army moved up the Red River in March. At the same time Maj. Gen. Frederick Steele, commanding Union forces in Arkansas, marched southward from Little Rock to support Banks's advance. To counter these measures Edmund Kirby Smith, Confederate Trans-Mississippi Department commander, called upon John B. Magruder to send cavalry reinforcements

THEN AND NOW

Ringgold Barracks, recaptured by John S. Ford and his Cavalry of the West in April 1864, is one of Texas's many nineteenth-century military posts. Located off US 83 on the east side of Rio Grande City, the fort was established after the Mexican War, occupied by both Union and Confederate forces during the Civil War, and was an active post of the U.S. Army until 1906. Among the surviving buildings are the old post hospital and the house allegedly occupied by Robert E. Lee when he commanded the Department of Texas in the late 1850s.

There are a number of other military posts in Texas that were abandoned when U.S. troops left Texas during the secession crisis. Most impressive of these is the Fort Davis National Historic Site in Jeff Davis County in West Texas. Established as a military post in 1854, the fort was evacuated by the federals in April 1861, occupied by the Confederates from the summer of 1861 to the late summer of 1862, and then unoccupied for the remainder of the war. When federal troops reoccupied the post in June 1867, much of the fort was in ruins. New construction produced substantial rock and adobe buildings, several of which have been restored. The site, operated today by the National Park Service, provides an excellent example of nineteenth-century frontier military life.

Among other Texas military posts that have buildings or artifacts associated with the Civil War are Fort Bliss at El Paso, Fort Duncan at Eagle Pass, Fort Mason at Mason, Fort McIntosh at Laredo, and Fort Belknap near Newcastle.

FORT DAVIS, TEXAS, HEAD-QUARTERS OF THE EIGHTH INFANTRY.—From a Sketch by a Government Draughtsman.—[See next Page.]

Fort Davis, Texas. From *Harper's Weekly*, March 16, 1861. CN 10126. *Courtesy Prints and Photographs Collection, Center for American History, University of Texas at Austin.*

from Texas to join Richard Taylor, Confederate commander in western Louisiana. Smith also instructed Sterling Price, Confederate commander in Arkansas, to send five thousand Arkansas and Missouri troops to join Taylor. With the remainder of his forces, Price was ordered to block Steele's move southward.[68]

As Banks moved into northwestern Louisiana, Richard Taylor concentrated his forces near the small crossroads town of Mansfield. Taylor had under his command two infantry divisions: one commanded by Missourian John G. Walker consisting of three Texas infantry brigades led by William R. Scurry, Thomas N. Waul, and Horace Randal; the other commanded by the Acadian Alfred Mouton consisting of a brigade of Louisianians led by Henry Gray and a brigade of Texans commanded by a French aristocrat, Camille Armand Jules Marie, the Prince de Polignac. In early April Taylor was joined at Mansfield by Tom Green's veteran

Camp Ford, Texas." Sketch by G. W. Simmons. From *Harper's Weekly*, March 4, 1865. *CN 03152. Courtesy Prints and Photographs Collection, Center for American History, University of Texas at Austin.*

Texas cavalry division and a newly formed Texas cavalry brigade led by Hamilton P. Bee.[69]

On the afternoon of April 8 Taylor attacked the advance units of Banks's army three miles south of Mansfield near Sabine Crossroads. In the battle Taylor's army drove the enemy back with heavy losses. Banks withdrew that evening toward Pleasant Hill, a small community fifteen miles to the south. There, on the next afternoon, Taylor, reinforced by troops from Sterling Price's army commanded by Thomas J. Churchill, attacked again. This time the federals, who had also been reinforced, pushed Taylor's army back. Even so, Banks ordered his army to continue its withdrawal toward the Red River. Taylor still hoped to deliver a punishing blow to Banks's army, but Kirby Smith, concerned about Steele's advance southward, sent Churchill's and Walker's divisions to join Sterling Price in southern Arkansas.[70]

With the remaining troops under his command, Taylor pursued Banks's retreating army. In the next six weeks a series of encounters between the two armies occurred. In one of these engagements, at Blair's Landing on April 12, one of Texas's most popular officers, Brig. Gen. Tom Green, was killed. In the last battle of the campaign, at Yellow Bayou, the Confederates sustained heavy losses, especially in Polignac's Texas Brigade.[71]

Although Taylor was unable to destroy Banks's army, he did keep the enemy from occupying northern Louisiana and eastern Texas. The price was high; total Confederate casualties for the Red River-Arkansas campaign were 4,300 men. Of these over half, 2,852, were Texans. Federal losses were 5,400 men.[72]

Several thousand Union soldiers were captured during the Red River campaign. Many of these were taken to Camp Ford, the Confederate prison several miles northeast of Tyler, Texas. Camp Ford was originally a training post but became a military prison in August 1863. At first the facility held only a few prisoners taken at Galveston, Sabine Pass, and in the Louisiana bayou country. The camp was enlarged in the spring of 1864 to house the Union troops captured in the Red River campaign. By the end of May 1864, there were over forty-five hundred inmates, making it the largest military prison west of the Mississippi. Some of the captives were later moved to Camp Groce, near Hempstead, a military prison established in June 1863. Although living conditions in both prisons were primitive, the death rate in the Texas camps was considerably lower than in other Confederate and Union facilities.[73]

The defeat of Banks in the Red River campaign did not mean the end of fighting in the Trans-Mississippi. Texans under the command of Sam Maxey assisted Missouri troops in capturing a large Union supply train at Poison Spring, Arkansas, in mid-April 1864. Later that month John G. Walker's Texas Division fought against Frederick Steele's Union army in a bloody engagement at Jenkins' Ferry, Arkansas, in which two Texas brigadiers, William R. Scurry and Horace Randal, were killed. During the late summer of 1864 several thousand Texans in Walker's and Polignac's infantry divisions and John A. Wharton's cavalry division were ordered to Arkansas to keep Union forces occupied while Sterling Price made a cavalry raid into Missouri. In September Brig. Gen.

THEN AND NOW

Camp Ford, located near Tyler, covered four to five acres of ground enclosed by a sixteen-foot-high wooden stockade. A large spring, which ran along the south wall of the stockade, provided water for the camp. Prisoners were required to build their own shelters, which they made from logs, brush, and blankets. Many prisoners dug holes in the ground for protection from the weather. Prior to the incarceration of the Red River campaign soldiers, conditions in the camp were not bad, but with the thousands of additional inmates in 1864 conditions deteriorated rapidly.

Following the end of the war the compound was destroyed by a Union cavalry detail. Little remains of the prison today although recent archaeological digs have uncovered outlines of the camp and various artifacts. A Texas historical marker on US 271, two miles northeast of Tyler, describes the prison. An interpretative kiosk and descriptive walking trails are scheduled to open in 1999.

Camp Groce, located on Leonard Groce's Liendo Plantation, two miles east of Hempstead, also began as a training camp. There are no physical remains of the camp, but a historical marker 2.9 miles east of Hempstead on US 290 provides some information. Liendo Plantation, with its sixteen-room Greek Revival mansion, is a Texas historic landmark listed in the National Register of Historic Places. Tours are offered the first Saturday of the month.

Richard Gano's Texas cavalry brigade, assisted by Stand Watie's Confederate Indians, made a sweep through Union-held Indian Territory and won a major victory at Cabin Creek.[74]

While these Texans were defending their homes and country in the Trans-Mississippi, many other Texans were fighting for the Confederacy east of the Mississippi. Hood's Texas Brigade, consisting of three regiments of Texas infantry and one regiment of Arkansas infantry, was one of the finest units in Robert E. Lee's Army of Northern Virginia. Commanded first by the volatile South Carolina-Texas politician Louis T. Wigfall, the Texas Brigade gained recognition under the leadership of John Bell Hood, a Kentuckian who considered Texas his adopted home. Hood succeeded Wigfall in early 1862 when the latter took his seat in the Confederate Senate. The Brigade attained a reputation for bravery and courage in the battles of Gaines Mill, Second Manassas (Bull Run),

and Sharpsburg (Antietam). At Sharpsburg the Texas Brigade suffered 64 percent casualties, twice that of the rest of the Confederate Army, in the bloodiest single day of the war. The First Texas
regiment of the brigade had 82.3 percent casualties, the highest of
any regiment, North or South, for one day in the war.[75]

Hood was promoted to major general in October 1862, and became division commander, but the brigade carried his name
throughout the remainder of the war. At the battle of Gettysburg
in July 1863, the brigade, then led by Washington County physician Jerome B. Robertson, was part of Hood's Division in the unsuccessful attack on the Union left flank at Little Round Top. In
the fighting Hood, Robertson, and three of the four regimental
commanders were wounded. The brigade itself suffered 54.3 percent casualties. Later that year the brigade was in the successful
Confederate attack at Chickamauga, Georgia, which broke the enemy line, leading to the defeat of William Rosecrans's Union
army.[76]

At Chickamauga Hood's Texans for the first time fought alongside other Texans serving in Braxton Bragg's Army of Tennessee.
These included four Texas regiments in Mathew D. Ector's infantry brigade, the Eighth Texas Cavalry (Terry's Texas Rangers)
and the Eleventh Texas Cavalry (both part of John A. Wharton's
cavalry division), the Seventh Texas Infantry commanded by Waco attorney Hiram Granbury, several consolidated Texas cavalry
regiments in James Deshler's brigade, and an artillery battery
commanded by Capt. James P. Douglas of Tyler.[77]

Hood's Brigade, commanded by Freestone County judge John
Gregg, rejoined Lee's Army of Northern Virginia in late spring
1864. In May the brigade took part in one of the most dramatic
moments of the war. Grant's Union army was attempting to push
Lee's troops aside in the Wilderness area to the west of the old
Virginia battlefield at Chancellorsville. The Texas Brigade arrived
just as other Rebel units were retreating under heavy Union as-
saults and a major break in the Confederate line appeared immi-
nent. Under the watchful eye of Robert E. Lee, who was on the
scene waving the brigade on with the admonition, "Texans Al-
ways Move Them," Gregg's infantry drove the enemy back and

stabilized the line, preventing a Union victory.[78]

As Lee's army fought to defend Virginia during the summer of 1864, the other main Confederate army, the Army of Tennessee, battled against William T. Sherman's forces around Atlanta. Once again Texans played a major role in the fighting. Ector's Brigade, Granbury's Brigade, and the Eighth and Eleventh Texas Cavalries were part of the army commanded by Joseph E. Johnston and later John Bell Hood. They were joined by a Texas cavalry brigade commanded by young Lawrence S. "Sul" Ross. When Atlanta fell to Sherman in early September, these Texas units served with Hood in the unsuccessful campaign to capture Nashville in November–December 1864.[79]

Defending the Confederacy in late 1863 and 1864 was particularly costly to Texas military commanders. Tom Green was killed at Blair's Landing, William R. Scurry and Horace Randal were mortally wounded at Jenkins' Ferry, John Bell Hood lost a leg at Chickamauga, Mathew D. Ector lost a leg at Atlanta, William H. Young (commander of the Eleventh Texas cavalry) was seriously wounded and captured north of Atlanta, Hiram Granbury was killed at Franklin, Tennessee, and John Gregg was killed near Richmond, Virginia.

Private George T. Brown, Company B, Third Texas Cavalry (Arizona Brigade).
Courtesy Lawrence T. Jones III, Austin.

5.
COLLAPSE OF THE
CONFEDERACY

DESPITE THE MANY sacrifices made by Texans and other Southerners, the effort to establish a Confederate nation came to an end in early 1865. On April 9, after four years of fighting against overwhelming odds, Robert E. Lee surrendered the Army of Northern Virginia at Appomattox Court House. Three days later the formal exchange of men and weapons took place. Among those in Lee's army were 617 members of Hood's Texas Brigade, the last of over five thousand Texans and Arkansans who had served in the brigade. After being paroled, these proud veterans began to make their way home to Texas and Arkansas.[80]

During the next month other Confederates capitulated. In late April Joseph E. Johnston surrendered what remained of the Army of Tennessee to William T. Sherman near Durham, North Carolina. On May 4 Richard Taylor surrendered Confederate troops in Alabama and Mississippi to E. R. S. Canby at Citronelle, Alabama.[81]

In Texas the initial reaction to reports of surrender was one of defiance. Kirby Smith, commander of the Trans-Mississippi Department, and John Bankhead Magruder, Confederate commander in Texas, both issued appeals to their troops to stand firm. In a proclamation to the people of Texas on April 27, Governor Murrah called upon Texans "to redeem the cause of the Confederate government from its present perils" and defend the state from the enemy. The editor of the Houston *Daily Telegraph*, E. H. Cushing, urged Texans to turn to guerrilla warfare if necessary to continue the struggle.[82]

This spirit of resistance soon began to wane as news of the surrenders in the East reached more Texans. Many agreed with Lee Nelms, a trooper in the Thirty-fourth Texas Cavalry camped near Hempstead that "there is [no] use in holding out any longer . . . it would be folly in us to fight on this side of the river now."[83]

On May 8, a Union staff officer, Col. John T. Sprague, brought Kirby Smith a letter from Maj. Gen. John Pope, commanding Union forces at St. Louis, outlining surrender terms similar to those accepted by Lee at Appomattox. Smith called a conference of Trans-Mississippi governors to meet again at Marshall to discuss the proposal. Present at the meeting were Governors Henry W. Allen of Louisiana, Harris Flanagin of Arkansas, and Thomas C. Reynolds of Missouri. Texas governor Pendleton Murrah was ill and unable to attend but was represented by Col. Guy M. Bryan. At the meeting the state executives rejected the Union terms and drafted their own proposals which provided for peace without formal surrender. These terms were unacceptable to Colonel Sprague, who returned to St. Louis to report the failure of his mission.[84]

At the time the Trans-Mississippi governors were meeting in Marshall, the last battle of the Civil War was being fought at Palmito Ranch, fifteen miles east of Brownsville. In a blinding rainstorm on the evening of May 11, 1865, Col. Theodore H. Barrett and a mixed force of African-American and white troops from the garrison on Brazos Santiago crossed over to the mainland. The next morning Barrett's troops skirmished with Confederates led by Capt. W. N. Robinson near Palmito Ranch and drove the Confederates back. The following day Col. John S. Ford with three hundred troops and a battery of artillery arrived. After several charges the Confederates broke the enemy line and the federals fell back in disorder to Boca Chica Strait which guarded the entrance to Brazos Island. Brig. Gen. James E. Slaughter, Confederate subdistrict commander who arrived on the scene at that moment, wanted the attack continued but Colonel Ford insisted his men were too exhausted to keep fighting. Union losses in the battle were between twenty-five and thirty killed and wounded and 113 captured. The Confederates reported only five casualties but the number is believed to have been higher.[85]

The engagement at Palmito Ranch was the last battle of the Civil War. A few days later several Union officers rode into Brownsville to confer with Gen. Slaughter and Colonel Ford. After some discussion the Confederates agreed that further resistance would be useless. Ford released his men who returned to their homes and families. Ford and his wife crossed over to Matamoros where they were guests of Mexican officials. Slaughter rode upriver to Eagle Pass where he joined a large group of Confederates heading for Mexico.[86]

Meanwhile Confederate authority in Texas was evaporating. On May 14 troops at Galveston attempted to desert but were persuaded by Col. Ashbel Smith to stay at their posts a few days longer. Kirby Smith gave orders for the concentration of troops at Houston, where he intended to make his headquarters. Before Smith arrived in Houston, however, many of the soldiers left their units and went home. Riots broke out in several Texas towns, including Houston, Galveston, Austin, and San Antonio. Soldiers, claiming that the government had not paid them for some time, began looting government warehouses. In Galveston small children stole military powder and cartridges, which they exploded in the streets for amusement. Confusion and chaos seemed to be everywhere. Washington County planter Thomas Affleck, a staunch supporter of the Confederacy, expressed the fears and concerns of many, declaring "the army has entirely disbanded, & are sacking as they go . . . We have no Govt. or country. God help us."[87]

THEN AND NOW

The Palmito Ranch battlefield is located approximately fifteen miles east of Brownsville. Part of the battlefield site is on privately owned land; other parts are owned by the U.S. Fish and Wildlife Service.

An historical marker describing the battlefield is located on State Highway 4, twelve miles east of Brownsville.

Major General Gordon Granger, carte de visite, March 1865. *Courtesy Lawrence T. Jones III, Austin.*

When Kirby Smith reached Houston on May 27, he found that most of the army had gone home. After appealing to Governor Murrah to use state troops to keep order, Smith issued a final address, justifying his actions and criticizing his soldiers for abandoning their posts. On June 2 Smith and General Magruder boarded the Union ship *Fort Jackson* in Galveston harbor and signed the documents surrendering what was left of the Trans-Mississippi Department.

During the next several weeks a number of Confederate political and military leaders, including Governors Murrah of Texas, Allen of Louisiana, Reynolds of Missouri, and Generals Smith, Magruder, Slaughter, Price, A. W. Terrell, Hamilton P. Bee, Thomas Hindman, and Jo Shelby crossed the Rio Grande and rode into Mexico. Eventually two thousand former Confederates located in Mexico, some briefly and others for years. More than one hundred Texans migrated to Brazil and other parts of Latin America.[88]

As former Confederate leaders departed, Union troops were arriving in Texas. In early June, Maj. Gen. Philip H. Sheridan, commanding the Military Division of the Southwest with headquarters in New Orleans, ordered Maj. Gen. Gordon Granger and eighteen hundred Union troops to proceed to Galveston as the advance party of federal occupying forces. Granger landed in Galveston on June 19. On that day he issued orders declaring that Lincoln's Emancipation Proclamation was in effect and that all slaves in Texas were free.[89]

Randolph Campbell points out that "it took time, of course, for Granger's order to become known across the state." Some owners

THEN AND NOW

There are numerous historical museums and archival collections in Texas that provide information pertaining to Texas's role in the Civil War. The Harold B. Simpson Confederate Research Center located on the campus of Hill Junior College, Hillsboro, Texas, contains more than three thousand volumes dealing with the Civil War, plus maps, photographs, correspondence, and dioramas. The Audie Murphy Memorial Gun Museum and Weapons Library, part of the Research Center, has historic firearms, edged weapons, and historical artifacts associated with the Civil War.

The Center for American History on the campus of the University of Texas at Austin, has an outstanding manuscript collection of diaries, letters, and papers of Texas Civil War soldiers and civilians. The Archives Division of the Texas State Library on Brazos Street in Austin has one hundred collections of Civil War manuscripts, including the correspondence of Ben and Henry McCulloch, papers of the governors, John S. Ford Papers, and executive record books.

The Galveston and Texas History Center, Rosenberg Library, 2310 Sealy Avenue, Galveston, has manuscripts, artifacts, and books pertaining to the Civil War, including the W. P. Ballinger Diary and Letters, John B. Magruder Papers, and Trueheart Family Papers.

called slaves together and read the proclamation. Others were slow to inform the freedmen. In most instances the former slaves greeted the news with rejoicing and celebration. Some left their former masters almost at once, others stayed on the plantation longer. Campbell notes that 51 percent of the slaves he studied remained with their former owners for at least one year after emancipation.[90]

Meanwhile, civil government was restored in Texas. President Andrew Johnson appointed Texas Unionist Andrew J. Hamilton provisional governor. Hamilton arrived in Texas in late July and, after stopovers at Galveston and Houston, reached the state capital on August 2. In his "Proclamation to the People of Texas," Hamilton declared all acts passed by the legislature during the war illegal and called for a new state constitution to be drafted by citizens loyal to the Union.[91]

The Civil War was over. Ahead lay the long, and sometimes bitter, weeks and months of Reconstruction.

CHRONOLOGY OF EVENTS

1860

November 6 Lincoln elected President

December 3 Address to People of Texas calling for state
convention

1861

January 8 Elections for delegates to state convention

28 State convention opens

February 1 State convention approves ordinance of secession

16 Twiggs surrenders federal property in Texas

23 People vote on secession ordinance

March 4 Convention canvasses vote of people

5 Convention passes ordinance uniting Texas with
Confederate States of America

16 Convention removes Houston from office

April 12 Confederates fire on Fort Sumter

May 5 Texas forces occupy federal forts in
Indian Territory

July 2 U.S. Navy initiates blockade of Galveston

27 John R. Baylor captures Ft. Fillmore, N.Mex.

August 10 Federals defeated at Wilson's Creek (Oak Hill)

| October | 23 | Sibley's Brigade leaves San Antonio for N.Mex. |

1862

February	21	Battle of Valverde, N.Mex.
March	7	Ben McCulloch killed at Pea Ridge, Ark.
	26–28	Battle of Glorieta Pass, N.Mex.
April	6	Albert Sidney Johnston killed at Shiloh, Tenn.
June	27	Hood's Brigade breaks enemy line at Gaines Mill
July	28	First Marshall Conference
	30	Hood's Brigade leads assault at 2nd Manassas
August	10	Battle of Nueces
	16–18	Federals attempt to capture Corpus Christi
September	17	Hood's Brigade in battle of Sharpsburg
	26	Union Navy destroys Fort Sabine
October	1–20	Great Hanging at Gainesville
	8	Federals occupy Galveston

1863

January	1	Confederates recapture Galveston
July	1–3	Battle of Gettysburg
	4	Vicksburg surrenders
August	15–18	Second Marshall Conference
September	8	Battle of Sabine Pass
	19–20	Battle of Chickamauga
November	2–6	Union forces occupy Brownsville

1864

March	19	Battle of Laredo
April	8	Battle of Mansfield
	9	Battle of Pleasant Hill
	12	Tom Green killed at Blair's Landing
July	20–28	Battles for Atlanta
	30	Confederates reoccupy Brownsville
October	12–20	Elm Creek Raid

November 30 Hiram Granbury killed at Franklin, Tenn.

1865

January 8 Battle of Dove Creek

April 9 Lee surrenders at Appomattox Court House

29 Joe Johnston surrenders in North Carolina

May 13 Battle of Palmito Ranch

June 2 Kirby Smith surrenders at Galveston

17 Andrew J. Hamilton appointed provisional governor of Texas

19 General Granger announces Emancipation Proclamation in effect in Texas

NOTES

1. *Journal of the Secession Convention of Texas, 1861*, ed. E. W. Winkler (Austin: Austin Printing Co., 1912), 25, 35–36; Walter L. Buenger, *Secession and the Union in Texas* (Austin: University of Texas Press, 1984), 144–149.

2. Delegates Richard Coke, John Ireland, O. M. Roberts, and James W. Throckmorton would later serve as governors. Future Confederate generals included Joseph L. Hogg, John Gregg, William P. Hardeman, Allison Nelson, Jerome B. Robertson, William R. Scurry, and John A. Wharton. For convention membership see Ralph A. Wooster, "An Analysis of the Membership of the Texas Secession Convention," *Southwestern Historical Quarterly*, 62 (Jan., 1959), 322–335 (cited hereafter as *SHQ*); and Wooster, *The Secession Conventions of the South* (Princeton: Princeton University Press, 1962), 124–129.

3. Llerena B. Friend, *Sam Houston: The Great Designer* (Austin: University of Texas Press, 1954), 338–339; Randolph B. Campbell, *Sam Houston and the American Southwest* (New York: Harper Collins, 1993), 155–156.

4. *The War of the Rebellion: A Compilation of the Official Records of the Union and Confederate Armies* (128 vols.; Washington, D.C.: Government Printing Office, 1880–1901), Ser. I, vol. I, 503–516 (cited hereafter as *Official Records, Armies*; unless indicated all entries are from Series I); Jeanne T. Heidler, "Embarrassing Situation: David E. Twiggs and the Surrender of United States Forces in Texas, 1861," *Military History of the Southwest*, 22 (Fall, 1991), 157–172.

5. *Journal of Secession Convention*, 321–324, 366–367; *Official Records, Armies*, I, 574–578; IV, 98–101; J. J. Bowden, *The Exodus of Federal Forces from Texas, 1861* (Austin: Eakin Press, 1986), 65–79.

6. Arthur James Lynn Fremantle, *The Fremantle Diary: Being the Journal of Lieutenant Colonel Arthur James Lynn Fremantle, Coldstream Guards, on His Three Months in the Southern States*, ed. Walter Lord (1863; reprint, Boston: Little, Brown Co., 1954), 58. Stephen B. Oates, *Confederate Cavalry West of the River* (Austin: University of Texas Press, 1961), 3–29, provides an excellent description of recruiting activities in Texas.

7. William A. Albaugh III, *Tyler, Texas, C. S. A.* (Harrisburg, Pa.: Stackpole Co., 1958), 11–12, 20–26, 270–271; Bill Winsor, *Texas in the Confederacy: Military Installations, Economy, and People* (Hillsboro: Hill Jr. College Press, 1963), 41–44; Vera Lea Dugas, "A Social and Economic History of Texas in the Civil War and Reconstruction Periods" (Ph.D. diss., University of Texas, 1963), 272–281.

8. Winsor, *Texas in the Confederacy,* 8–38; Harold B. Simpson, *Hood's Texas Brigade: Lee's Grenadier Guard* (Waco: Texian Press, 1970), 20–21, 34–35; J. P. Blessington, *The Campaigns of Walker's Texas Division* (1875; reprint, Austin: State House Press, 1994), 21–22.

9. *Official Records, Armies,* III, 104–107, 109; Thomas W. Cutrer, *Ben McCulloch and the Frontier Military Tradition* (Chapel Hill: University of North Carolina Press, 1993), 193–244; Douglas Hale, *The Third Texas Cavalry in the Civil War* (Norman: University of Oklahoma Press, 1993), 50–69.

10. Cutrer, *Ben McCulloch,* 303–309; William L. Shea and Earl J. Hess, *Pea Ridge: Civil War Campaign in the West* (Chapel Hill: University of North Carolina Press, 1992), 88–260.

11. *Official Records, Armies,* IV, 5–22; Jerry Don Thompson, *Colonel John Robert Baylor: Texas Indian Fighter and Confederate Soldier* (Hillsboro: Hill Jr. College Press, 1991), 24–26, 45–46.

12. For more on the New Mexico campaign see Martin H. Hall, *Sibley's New Mexico Campaign* (Austin: University of Texas Press, 1960); Martin H. Hall, *The Confederate Army of New Mexico* (Austin: Presidial Press, 1978); Donald S. Frazier, *Blood and Treasure: Confederate Empire in the Southwest* (College Station: Texas A&M University Press, 1995); Jerry Thompson, *Confederate General of the West: Henry Hopkins Sibley* (College Station: Texas A&M University Press, 1996); Don E. Alberts (ed.), *Rebels on the Rio Grande: The Civil War Journal of A. B. Peticolas* (Albuquerque: Merit Press, 1993); Don E. Alberts, *The Battle of Glorieta: Union Victory in the West* (College Station: Texas A&M University Press, 1998); and Thomas S. Edrington and John Taylor, *The Battle of Glorieta Pass: A Gettysburg in the West, March 26–28, 1862* (Albuquerque: University of New Mexico Press, 1998).

13. For Johnston's death see Charles P. Roland, *Albert Sidney Johnston: Soldier of Three Republics* (Austin: University of Texas Press, 1964), 336–340; George W. Baylor, *Into the Far, Wild Country: True Tales of the Old Southwest,* ed. Jerry D. Thompson (El Paso: Texas Western Press, 1996), 220–228; Wiley Sword, *Shiloh: Bloody April* (New York: William Morrow & Co., 1974), 442–446. The most recent study of the battle itself is Larry J. Daniel, *Shiloh: The Battle that Changed the Civil War* (New York: Simon & Schuster, 1997).

14. *Official Records, Armies,* X, pt. 1, 494–504, 508–510, 560–564, 626–627; J. K. P. Blackburn, "Reminiscences of the Terry Rangers," *Terry Texas Ranger Trilogy* (Austin: State House Press, 1996), 110–122; L. B. Giles, "Terry's Texas Rangers," ibid., 23–26; Joseph E. Chance, *The Second Texas Infantry: From Shiloh to Vicksburg* (Austin: Eakin Press, 1984), 21–41.

15. Edward T. Cotham Jr., *Battle on the Bay: The Civil War Struggle for Galveston* (Austin: University of Texas Press, 1998), 31–56. The best account of the Confederate coastline defense is Alwyn Barr, "Texas Coastal Defense, 1861–1865," *SHQ,* 65 (July, 1961), 1–31.

16. *Official Records, Armies*, IX, 618–625; Norman Delaney, "Corpus Christi—The Vicksburg of Texas," *Civil War Times Illustrated*, 16 (July, 1977), 4–9, 44–48; Bill Walraven, *Corpus Christi: The History of a Texas Seaport* (Sun Valley, Calif.: American Historical Press, 1997), 50, 52–53.

17. *Official Records, Armies*, XV, 143–147; *Official Records of the Union and Confederate Navies in the War of the Rebellion* (31 vols.; Washington, D.C.: Government Printing Office, 1899–1908), Ser. I, XIX, 227–229 (cited hereafter as *Official Records, Navies*; unless indicated all entries are from Series I); W. T. Block, *History of Jefferson County, Texas, from Wilderness to Reconstruction* (Nederland: Nederland Printing, 1976), 98–104; W. T. Block, "The Civil War Comes to Jefferson County, Texas," *Blue and Gray Magazine*, 4 (Sept., 1986), 14–15.

18. Charles C. Cumberland, "The Confederate Loss and Recapture of Galveston, 1862–1863," *SHQ*, 51 (Oct., 1947), 110–114; Cotham, *Battle on the Bay*, 58–67; William Pitt Ballinger, Diary, Ballinger Papers (Center for American History, University of Texas at Austin), 79.

19. *Official Records, Navies*, XIX, 404, 409–410; Cotham, *Battle on the Bay*, 69–72.

20. Paul D. Casdorph, *Prince John Magruder: His Life and Campaigns* (New York: John Wiley & Sons, 1996), 223–228; Cotham, *Battle on the Bay*, 105–112.

21. Donald S. Frazier, *Cottonclads! The Battle of Galveston and the Defense of the Texas Coast* (Fort Worth: Ryan Place Publishers, 1996), 48–63.

22. Barr, "Texas Coastal Defense," 14–16; Frazier, *Cottonclads!*, 65–73; Cotham, *Battle on the Bay*, 113–130.

23. Cotham, *Battle on the Bay*, 125–126; *Official Records, Navies*, XIX, 473–474. For more on Leon Smith see James M. Day, "Leon Smith: Confederate Mariner," *East Texas Historical Journal*, 3 (Mar., 1965), 34–49.

24. Cotham, *Battle on the Bay*, 127–132; *Official Records, Navies*, XIX, 474–475; Cumberland, "Confederate Loss and Recapture of Galveston," 124–126; Virgil Carrington Jones, "The Battle of Galveston Harbor," *Civil War Times Illustrated*, 5 (Feb., 1967), 33–38.

25. Raphael Semmes, *Memoirs of Service Afloat, During the War Between the States* (Baltimore: Kelly, Piet, and Co., 1869), 542–550; W. T. Block, "The Swamp Angels: A History of Spaight's 11th Battalion, Texas Volunteers, Confederate States Army," *East Texas Historical Journal*, 30 (Spring, 1992), 49–50.

26. Block, *History of Jefferson County*, 108; Andrew Forest Muir, "Dick Dowling and the Battle of Sabine Pass," *Civil War History*, 4 (Dec., 1958), 411–412.

27. Kurk Henry Hackemer, "Strategic Dilemma: Civil-Military Friction and the Texas Coastal Campaign of 1863," *Military History of the West*, 26 (Fall, 1996), 188–201; Casdorph, *Prince John Magruder*, 252–253; Fred Harvey Harrington, *Fighting Politician: Major General N. P. Banks* (Philadelphia: University of Pennsylvania Press, 1948), 128.

28. Barr, "Texas Coastal Defense," 23–24. There is some disagreement on the number of Union troops. *Official Records, Armies*, XXVI, pt. 1, 288–289, gives the number as five thousand. *Official Records, Navies*, XX, 515, reports four thousand troops.

29. Frank X. Tolbert, *Dick Dowling at Sabine Pass* (New York: McGraw-Hill, 1962),

92; Harold B. Simpson "The Battle of Sabine Pass," in Seymour Connor, et. al., *Battles of Texas* (Waco: Texian Press, 1967), 152–155.

30. Muir, "Dick Dowling and Sabine Pass," 418; Frazier, *Cottonclads!*, 110–111.

31. For Dowling's report of the battle see *Official Records, Armies*, XXVI, pt. 1, 311–312; for Franklin's report, ibid., 294–297; for Crocker's report, ibid., 301–302. Banks's biographer, Fred Harvey Harrington, *Fighting Politician*, 131, states "sound in outline, this campaign was thrown away by bad planning, the lack of army-navy cooperation, and a series of incredible mistakes."

32. Muir, "Dick Dowling and Sabine Pass," 420–421. Muir ranked Sabine Pass with the defense of the Alamo and the battle of San Jacinto for bravery and military results. Ibid., 412.

33. Block, *History of Jefferson County*, 115–116. Fort Manhassett was named for a federal schooner that had beached nearby in a storm.

34. James A. Irby, *Backdoor at Bagdad: The Civil War on the Rio Grande* (El Paso: Texas Western Press, 1977), 29–30; Jerry Thompson, *A Wild and Vivid Land: An Illustrated History of the South Texas Border* (Austin: Texas State Historical Association, 1997), 109–110; Hackemer, "Strategic Dilemma," 206–207.

35. Lester N. Fitzhugh, "Saluria, Fort Esperanza, and Military Operations on the Texas Coast, 1861–1864," *SHQ*, 61 (July, 1957), 95–97; Jerry D. Thompson, *Mexican Texans in the Union Army* (El Paso: Texas Western Press, 1986), 15–16.

36. David S. Kennard to Father and Mother, Nov. 28, 1861, quoted in Cotham, *Battle on the Bay*, 41; Fremantle, *Diary*, 62; Eliza McHatton-Ripley, *From Flag to Flag: A Woman's Adventures and Experiences in the South during the War, in Mexico, and in Cuba* (New York: D. Appleton & Co., 1896), 101.

37. McHatton-Ripley, *From Flag to Flag*, 97, 99; Amelia Barr, *All the Days of My Life: An Autobiography* (New York: D. Appleton & Co., 1917), 243.

38. Marshall *Texas Republican*, Mar. 8, 1862, Jan. 19, Apr. 11, 1863; Sallie Haltom, "My Life in Tarrant County and Other Parts of Texas," *SHQ*, 60 (July, 1956), 102; Robert P. Felgar, "Texas in the War for Southern Independence, 1861–1865" (Ph.D. diss., University of Texas, 1935), 410–412; McHatton-Ripley, *From Flag to Flag*, 98; Paul A. Levengood, "In the Absence of Scarcity: The Civil War Prosperity of Houston, Texas," *SHQ*, 101 (Apr., 1998), 422–424. In his article Levengood points out that the Bayou City suffered few of the shortages reported elsewhere.

39. Kate Stone, *Brokenburn: The Journal of Kate Stone, 1861–1868*, ed. John Q. Anderson (Baton Rouge: Louisiana State University Press, 1955), xx–xxiii, 237, 358; Mary Elizabeth Massey, *Refugee Life in the Confederacy* (Baton Rouge: Louisiana State University Press, 1964), 6, 36, 38, 92–93, 123–124; Alwyn Barr, "The 'Queen City of the Gulf' Held Hostage: The Impact of War on Confederate Galveston," *Military History of the West*, 27 (Fall, 1997), 128–130.

40. There are numerous accounts of the Mexican trade. See James W. Daddysman, *The Matamoros Trade: Confederate Commerce, Diplomacy, and Intrigue* (Newark Del.: The University of Delaware Press, 1984); Robert W. Delaney, "Matamoros, Port for Texas During the Civil War," *SHQ*, 58 (Apr., 1955), 473–487; Ronnie C. Tyler, "Cotton on the Border, 1861–1865," ibid., 73 (Apr., 1970), 456–477; Fredericka Meiners, "The Texas Border Cotton Trade, 1862–1863," *Civil War History*, 23 (Dec.,

1977), 193–206.

41. L. Tuffly Ellis, "Maritime Commerce on the Far Western Gulf Coast, 1861–1865," *SHQ*, 77 (Oct., 1973), 197. Alwyn Barr, "'Queen City of the Gulf' Held Hostage," 126, points out, however, that slower ships did not attempt to enter Confederate ports. He observes that the number of ships entering Galveston during the war never approached the prewar numbers. See also Marcus W. Price, "Ships that Tested the Blockade of the Gulf Ports, 1861–1865," *American Neptune*, 11 (Oct., 1951), 262–263; Robert W. Glover, "The West Gulf Blockade, 1861–1865: An Evaluation" (Ph.D. diss., North Texas State University, 1974), 143–148, 242–244; W. T. Block, *"Schooner Sail to Starboard": Confederate Blockade-Running on the Louisiana-Texas Coast Lines* (Woodville, Tex.: Dogwood Press, 1997).

42. James L. Nichols, *The Confederate Quartermaster in the Trans-Mississippi* (Austin: University of Texas Press, 1964), 58–75; Robert L. Kerby, *Kirby Smith's Confederacy: The Trans-Mississippi South, 1863–1865* (New York: Columbia University Press, 1972), 138–139, 152–160, 201–202.

43. David P. Smith, "Conscription and Conflict on the Texas Frontier," *Civil War History*, 36 (Sept., 1990), 252–254, 257–261; *Official Records, Armies*, XXXIV, pt. 2, 1093–1095; pt. 3, 739–741, 747–750.

44. Francis R. Lubbock, *Six Decades in Texas; or, Memoirs of Francis R. Lubbock, Governor of Texas in War Time, 1861–1863*, ed. C. W. Raines (Austin: Ben C. Jones & Co., 1900), 388–394, 493–501. For more on the Confederate-Texas relations see the excellent study by Fredericka Ann Meiners, "The Texas Governorship, 1861–1865: Biography of An Office" (Ph.D. diss., Rice University, 1974).

45. James Marten, *Texas Divided: Loyalty and Dissent in the Lone Star State, 1856–1874* (Lexington: University Press of Kentucky, 1990), 33–52; Claude Elliott, *Leathercoat: The Life of James W. Throckmorton* (San Antonio: Standard Printing Co., 1938), 63–98; Ralph A. Wooster, "Ben H. Epperson: East Texas Lawyer, Legislator, and Civic Leader," *East Texas Historical Journal*, 5 (Mar., 1967), 29–42; David Paul Smith, *Frontier Defense in the Civil War: Texas' Rangers and Rebels* (College Station: Texas A&M University Press, 1992), 58.

46. Marten, *Texas Divided*, 59–60, 72–74; Randolph B. Campbell, "George T. Whitmore: East Texas Unionist," *East Texas Historical Journal*, 28 (Spring, 1990), 20–21; Ron Tyler, et. al., *The New Handbook of Texas*, (6 vols.; Austin: Texas State Historical Association, 1996), I, 849; V, 80–81, 113, 126–127; VI, 625, 948.

47. Campbell, *Sam Houston*, 158–159; David Paul Smith (ed.), "Civil War Letters of Sam Houston," *SHQ*, 81 (Apr., 1978), 422, 424; Chance, *The Second Texas Infantry*, 5.

48. Marten, *Texas Divided*, 63–64, 69–71, 79–80; Noah Smithwick, *The Evolution of a State; or, Recollections of Old Texas Days* (1900; reprint, Austin: Texas State Historical Association, 1983), 249–263; James Marten, "A Wearying Experience: Texas Refugees in New Orleans, 1862–1865," *Louisiana History*, 28 (Feb., 1987), 343–353; *New Handbook of Texas*, V, 445, 562–563; VI, 176.

49. Frank H. Smyrl, "Texans in the Union Army, 1861–1865," *SHQ*, 65 (Oct., 1961), 234–243; Jerry Don Thompson, *Vaqueros in Blue and Gray* (Austin: Presidal Press, 1976), 81; Ronald N. Gray. "Edmund J. Davis: Radical Republican and Reconstruction Governor of Texas" (Ph.D. diss., Texas Tech University, 1976), 31–40.

50. Jerry D. Thompson, *Mexican Texans in the Union Army* (El Paso: Texas Western Press, 1986), 13–17; James Marten, "John L. Haynes: A Southern Dissenter in Texas," *Southern Studies*, New Series, 1 (Fall, 1990), 257–279.

51. John L. Waller, *Colossal Hamilton of Texas: A Biography of Andrew Jackson Hamilton* (El Paso: Texas Western Press, 1968), 34–58; Richard N. Current, *Lincoln's Loyalists: Union Soldiers from the Confederacy* (Boston: Northeastern University Press, 1992), 95–106.

52. Claude Elliott, "Union Sentiment in Texas, 1861–1865," *SHQ*, 51 (Apr., 1947), 450.

53. Terry G. Jordan, *German Seed in Texas Soil: Immigrant Farmers in Nineteenth Century Texas* (Austin: University of Texas Press, 1966), 182–185; Marten, *Texas Divided*, 119–120.

54. Quoted by Robert W. Shook, "The Battle of the Nueces, August 10, 1862," *SHQ*, 66 (July, 1962), 41.

55. There are numerous accounts of the "great Gainesville hanging." The most thorough and scholarly is Richard B. McCaslin, *Tainted Breeze: The Great Hanging at Gainesville, Texas, 1862* (Baton Rouge: Louisiana State University Press, 1994).

56. Smith, *Frontier Defense in the Civil War*, 64–65, 79–80, 112–128; Richard B. McCaslin, "Dark Corner of the Confederacy: James G. Bourland and the Border Regiment," *Military History of the West*, 24 (Spring, 1994), 57–70.

57. Judith N. McArthur, "Myth, Reality and Anomaly: The Complex World of Rebecca Haggerty," *East Texas Historical Journal*, 24 (Fall, 1986), 18–32; Joleene Maddox Snider, "Sarah Devereux: A Study in Southern Feminity," *SHQ*, 97 (Jan., 1994), 492–502; Drew Gilpin Faust, *Southern Stories: Slaveholders in Peace and War* (Columbia: University of Missouri Press, 1992), 174–192; Seymour V. Connor (ed.), *Dear America: Some Letters of Orange Cicero and Mary America (Aiken) Connor* (Austin: Jenkins Publishing Co., 1971), 30–34, 39–55.

58. *New Handbook of Texas*, V, 275, 943–944; Block, *History of Jefferson County*, 114. For more on the role of Southern women in the war see Drew Gilpin Faust, *Mothers of Invention: Women of the Slaveholding South in the American Civil War* (Chapel Hill: University of North Carolina Press, 1996).

59. Randolph B. Campbell, *An Empire for Slavery: The Peculiar Institution in Texas* (Baton Rouge: Louisiana State University Press, 1989), 247.

60. Smith, *Frontier Defense in the Civil War*, 83–85; David Paul Smith, "Frontier Defense and the Cooke County Raid, 1863," *West Texas Historical Association Year Book*, 64 (Oct., 1988), 39–41.

61. David Paul Smith, "The Elm Creek Raid, 1864: State and Confederate Defense and Response," *Military History of the Southwest*, 19 (Fall, 1989), 121–136; Kenneth Neighbours, "Elm Creek Raid in Young County, 1864," *West Texas Historical Association Year Book*, 40 (Oct., 1964), 83–89.

62. Marilynne Howsley, "Forting Up on the Texas Frontier During the Civil War," *West Texas Historical Association Year Book*, 17 (Oct., 1941), 71–76; David Marshall, "A Civilian Fort on the Confederate Frontier: Samuel and Susan Newcomb at Ft. Davis on the Clear Fork of the Brazos," *ibid.*, 61 (Oct., 1985), 74–87; William C. Pool, "The Battle of Dove Creek," *SHQ*, 53 (Apr., 1950), 367–385.

63. *Official Records, Armies*, XLI, pt. 1, 939–943; *New Handbook of Texas*, I, 34. The second battle of Adobe Walls, between buffalo hunters and Plains Indians, occurred on June 27, 1874. There were other instances during the Civil War in which Indian attacks or raids took the lives of Texans. George W. Baylor, in his *Into the Far Wild Country*, cited earlier, points out that in August 1861 Lt. Reuben Mays and a squad from Company D, Second Texas Rifles, along with a number of citizens of Fort Davis, were massacred by Mescalero Apaches in a canyon in the Big Bend. Baylor, ibid., 208–219.

64. John Salmon Ford, *Rip Ford's Texas*, ed. Stephen B. Oates (Austin: University of Texas Press, 1963), 355–363; Thompson, *Vaqueros in Blue and Gray*, 101–116.

65. Oates (ed.), *Rip Ford's Texas*, 363–366; W. T. Hughes, *Rebellious Ranger: Rip Ford and the Old Southwest* (Norman: University of Oklahoma Press, 1964), 222–224.

66. Hughes, *Rebellious Ranger: Rip Ford and the Old Southwest*, 227–230; Oates (ed.), *Rip Ford's Texas*, 369–382.

67. Ludwell H. Johnson, *Red River Campaign: Politics and Cotton in the Civil War* (Baltimore: Johns Hopkins Press, 1958), 41–48.

68. *Official Records, Armies*, XXXIV, pt. 1, 479, 494, pt. 2, 1024–1027; Johnson, *Red River Campaign*, 81–87.

69. *Official Records, Armies*, XXXIV, pt. 1, 514–515, 518; J. P. Blessington, *The Campaigns of Walker's Texas Division* (1875; reprint, Austin: State House Press, 1994), 169–181; Alwyn Barr, *Polignac's Texas Brigade* (1964; new edition, College Station: Texas A&M University Press, 1998), 21–22, 39–40.

70. *Official Records, Armies*, XXXIV, pt. 1, 181–185, 534–536, 560–572, 606–607; Richard Taylor, *Destruction and Reconstruction: Personal Experiences of the Late War*, ed. Richard Harwell (1879; reprint, New York: Longmans, Green, and Co., 1955), 194–213; T. Michael Parrish, *Richard Taylor: Prince of Dixie* (Chapel Hill: University of North Carolina Press, 1992), 335–372; Harrington, *Fighting Politician*, 153–159.

71. Taylor, *Destruction and Reconstruction*, 214–232; Barr, *Polignac's Texas Brigade*, 43–47; Johnson, *Red River Campaign*, 206–276; Anne J. Bailey, *Between the Enemy and Texas: Parsons's Texas Cavalry Brigade in the Civil War* (Fort Worth: Texas Christian University Press, 1989), 181–189.

72. Alwyn Barr, "Texas Losses in the Red River Campaign, 1864," *Texas Military History*, 3 (Summer, 1963), 103–110.

73. F. Lee Lawrence and Robert W. Glover, *Camp Ford, C.S.A.: The Story of Union Prisoners in Texas* (Austin: Texas Civil War Committee, 1964), 3–21, 72–73; Robert W. Glover and Randal B. Gilbert, "Camp Ford, Tyler, Texas—The Largest Confederate Prison Camp West of the Mississippi River," *Chronicles of Smith County*, 28 (Winter, 1989), 16–32; Leon Mitchell Jr., "Camp Ford: Confederate Prison," *SHQ*, 66 (July, 1962), 1–6, 11–13; Lonnie R. Speer, *Portals to Hell: Military Prisons of the Civil War* (Mechanicsburg, Pa.: Stackpole Books, 1997), 129–131, 215–218, 333.

74. *Official Records, Armies*, XXXIV, pt. 1, 816–818; Blessington, *Campaigns of Walker's Texas Division*, 249–255; Barr, *Polignac's Brigade*, 49–51; Kerby, *Kirby Smith's Confederacy*, 331–355; Louise Horton, *Samuel Bell Maxey: A Biography* (Austin: University of Texas Press, 1974), 37–41.

75. The definite account of the Hood Brigade is the four-volume study by Col.

Harold B. Simpson, *Hood's Texas Brigade in Poetry and Song* (Waco: Texian Press, 1968); *Hood's Texas Brigade: Lee's Grenadier Guard* (Waco: Texian Press, 1970); *Hood's Texas Brigade in Reunion and Memory* (Waco: Texian Press, 1974); and *Hood's Texas Brigade: A Compendium* (Waco: Texian Press, 1977). References hereafter are to *Hood's Texas Brigade: Lee's Grenadier Guard*, which is the narrative describing the brigade's role in the war.

76. Simpson, *Hood's Texas Brigade*, 268–332.

77. James M. McCaffrey, *This Band of Heroes: Granbury's Texas Brigade, C.S.A.* (Austin: Eakin Press, 1965), 65–68; Peter Cozzens, *This Terrible Sound: The Battle of Chickamauga* (Urbana: University of Illinois Press, 1992), 135, 544–553.

78. Gordon Rhea, *The Battle of the Wilderness, May 5–6, 1864* (Baton Rouge: Louisiana State University Press, 1994), 283–306; Douglas Southall Freeman, *Lee's Lieutenants*, (3 vols.; New York: Charles Scribner's Sons, 1942–1944), III, 344–356; Robert K. Krick, "'Lee to the Rear', the Texans Cried," in Gary W. Gallagher (ed.), *The Wilderness Campaign* (Chapel Hill: University of North Carolina Press, 1997), 160–200.

79. For the Atlanta campaign see Albert Castel, *Decision in the West: The Atlanta Campaign of 1864* (Lawrence: University Press of Kansas, 1992). For Hood's Tennessee campaign see Wiley Sword, *The Confederacy's Last Hurrah: Spring Hill, Franklin and Nashville* (Lawrence: University Press of Kansas, 1992).

80. Harold B. Simpson, "Hood's Brigade at Appomattox," *Texana*, 3 (Spring, 1965), 1–19. In another article, "East Texas Companies in Hood's Brigade," *East Texas Historical Journal*, 3 (Mar., 1965), 13, Simpson states that of 4,300 Texans who had served in the brigade 476 were present at Appomattox.

81. Four hundred forty Texans in Granbury's Brigade were among the Confederates surrendering to Sherman. McCaffrey, *This Band of Heroes*, 156.

82. Murrah's proclamation quoted in Allan Ashcraft, "Texas: 1860–1866. The Lone Star State in the Civil War" (Ph.D. diss., Columbia University, 1960), 246; *Official Records, Armies*, XLVIII, pt. 2, 1282–1285; Emory Thomas, "Rebel Nationalism: E. H. Cushing and the Confederate Experience," *SHQ*, 73 (Jan., 1970), 349.

83. Robert S. Weddle, *Plow-Horse Cavalry: The Caney Creek Boys of the Thirty-fourth Texas* (Austin: Madrona Press, 1974), 158.

84. Meiners, "Texas Governorship," 376–377; Kerby, *Kirby Smith's Confederacy*, 418–419.

85. *Official Records, Armies*, XLVIII, pt. 1, 265–268; Thompson, *A Wild and Vivid Land*, 115–116; Oates (ed.), *Rip Ford's Texas*, 389–393; Noah Andre Trudeau, *Out of the Storm: The End of the Civil War, April–June 1865* (Boston: Little, Brown and Co., 1994), 301–308.

86. Confederate veterans of Palmito Ranch would later claim that prior to the battle they were not aware the war had ended. In a footnote to *Rip Ford's Texas*, p. 396, Stephen Oates says Ford and his lieutenants did not know about Appomattox at the time of the battle, but Jerry Thompson, *A Wild and Vivid Land*, 115, states that news of Lee's surrender had reached Brownsville before the battle at Palmito Ranch.

87. Elizabeth Silverthorne, *Ashbel Smith of Texas: Pioneer, Patriot, Statesman,*

1805–1886 (College Station: Texas A&M University Press, 1982), 167; Cotham, *Battle on the Bay*, 180–181; W. Buck Yearns (ed.), *From Richmond to Texas: The 1865 Journey Home of Confederate Senator Williamson S. Oldham* (Dayton, Ohio: Morningside House, Inc., 1998), 97–99; Thomas Affleck to John Anderson, May 23, 1865, Affleck Papers (Department of Manuscripts and Archives, Louisiana State University).

88. William W. White, *The Confederate Veteran* (Tuscaloosa, Ala.: Confederate Publishing Co., 1962), 61–64; Alexander W. Terrell, *From Texas to Mexico and the Court of Maximilian* (Dallas: Book Club of Texas, 1933), 3–10.

89. Robert W. Shook, "Federal Occupation and Administration of Texas, 1865–1870" (Ph.D. diss., North Texas State University, 1970), 76–78; William C. Richter, *The Army in Texas During Reconstruction* (College Station: Texas A&M University Press, 1987), 11–16.

90. Campbell, *An Empire for Slavery*, 249–250.

91. Waller, *Colossal Hamilton*, 60–64; Richter, *Army in Texas During Reconstruction*, 21–23. For more on Andrew J. Hamilton's influence in the Reconstruction process see William C. Harris, *With Charity for All: Lincoln and the Restoration of the Union* (Lexington: University Press of Kentucky, 1997), 88, 92–95.

ADDITIONAL READING

Governor O. M. Roberts's narrative in Volume XI, *Confederate Military History*, ed. Clement Evans (Atlanta: Confederate Publishing Co., 1899) is a thorough account of Texas's role in the Civil War, written by the man who chaired the Texas Secession Convention and later commanded the Eleventh Texas Infantry in the Louisiana campaigns. Ralph A. Wooster, *Texas and Texans in the Civil War* (Austin: Eakin Press, 1995) is a recent account that parallels Roberts's earlier work and incorporates modern scholarship on the subject. *Lone Star Blue and Gray*, ed. Ralph A. Wooster (Austin: Texas State Historical Association, 1995) is a collection of sixteen essays written by recognized authorities on specific aspects of Texas involvement in the war. B. P. Gallaway (ed.), *Texas, The Dark Corner of the Confederacy* (3rd ed., Lincoln: University of Nebraska Press, 1994), consists of eyewitness accounts of Civil War Texas and Texans. It also contains an outstanding bibliographical essay by one of the state's most able historians, Alwyn Barr. A recent publication, by Carl Moneyhon and Bobby Roberts, *Portraits of Conflict: A Photographic History of the Civil War in Texas* (Fayetteville: University of Arkansas Press, 1998), provides a visual picture of Texas and Texans in the Civil War. Bill Groneman, *Battlefields of Texas*, with maps and graphics by Rod Timanus (Plano: Republic of Texas Press, 1998), gives additional information on Civil War battle sites in Texas.

The published material on specific aspects of Texas's role in the war is voluminous. See the works cited in the notes for this book and in the essay by Alwyn Barr.

INDEX

(Pages with illustrations are indicated in **boldface**)

Fort Sabine: 14, 21, 65
Fort Sumter: 5, 64
"forting up": 47–48
Fourth Arkansas Cavalry: 7
Fourth Texas Infantry: 6
Franklin, William B.: 22, 24, 26
Franklin, battle of: 57, 65
Fredericksburg, Texas: 40
Freeman plantation: 36
Fremantle, Arthur: 5, 32
frontier, defense of: 47–49
Frontier District: 47
Frontier Organization: 34, 35
Frontier Regiment: 47

G

Gaines Mill, battle of: 56, 65
Gainesville, Texas: 43, 65
Galveston, Texas: 6, 13, 14, 20, 21, 31, 33, 61, 62, 63–66; captured by Union navy 15; recaptured by Confederates, 17–20
Galveston County Historical Commission: 21
Gano, Richard: 55
Gano's Cavalry Brigade: 55
Georgia: 1, 31
Germans: 40–41
Gettysburg, battle of: 56, 65
Gilmer, Texas: 7
Glorieta Pass, battle of: 8, 65
Granbury, Hiram: 57, 65
Granbury's Brigade: 57
Granger, Gordon: 62
Granite City: 14, 26
Grant, U. S.: 9
Gray, Henry: 52
Grayson County: 43, 44
Green, Tom: 8, 17, 19, 52, 54, 57, 65
Greer, Elkanah: 8, 34
Gregg, John: 56, 57, 67n
Griffin, W. H.: 22
Grimes County: 6
Groce, Leonard: 55

H

Hagerty, Rebecca: 44
Hamilton, Andrew J.: 40, 41, 63, 66
hanging: 43
Hardeman, William P.: 67n
Harold B. Simpson Confederate Research Center: 63
Harriet Lane: 19–20
Harris County: 6

Harrison County: 6, 36
Hatteras: 20–21
Havana, Cuba: 33–34
Haynes, John L: 28, 39
Hébert, Paul O.: 13–14
Hempstead, Texas: 6, 37, 54–55, 60
Hendley Building: 21
Herron, Francis J.: 49
Hill Junior College: 63
Hillsboro, Texas: 63
Hindman, Thomas: 62
Hispanic Confederates: 12
historical markers: 3, 7, 15, 21, 26, 43, 48, 55, 61
Hobby, A. M.: 14
Hogg, Joseph L.: 67n
Hood, John Bell: 55–56, 57
Hood's Texas Brigade: 6, 55–57, 59, 65; monument, 3
Holt, Alfred E.: 49
Houston, Sam: 1, 2, 35–36, 37, 38, 39, 40, 64
Houston, Sam, Jr.: 9
Houston, Texas: 22, 32, 61, 63
Huntsville, Texas: 6
Hutchinson County: 48

I

impressment: 34
Indianola, Texas: 26, 28, 31, 33
Indian Point: 26
Indians: 47–49, 55
Indian Territory: 36
Ireland, John: 14, 67n

J

Jeff Davis County: 51
Jefferson, Texas: 7, 36, 51
Jefferson County: 25
Jenkins' Ferry, battle of: 54, 57
John F. Carr: 20
Johnson, Andrew: 63
Johnston, Albert Sidney: 9, 37, 65; statue of, 3
Johnston, Joseph E.: 57, 59, 66
Josiah H. Bell: 21

K

Kennard, David: 31
Kentucky: 37
Kickapoos: 48
Kinney County: 43
Kiowas: 48

Stone, Kate: 33
Strand National Historic District: 21
Swenson, Swen Magnus: 37

T

Tamaulipas, Mexico: 50
Taylor, Richard: 52–53, 59
Taylor, Zachary: 14
Taylor's Bayou: 14
Tegener, Fritz: 42
Teich, Frank: 36, 43
Tejanos. 39
Tennessee: 31, 37
Terrell, A. W.: 62
Terry, Benjamin F · 10
Terry's Texas Rangers: 10, 57; Memorial, 3.
   See also Eighth Texas Cavalry
Texans: in Arkansas campaigns, 7–8, 51–53;
   in Atlanta campaign, 49; in
   Chickamauga battle, 48; in Confederate
   service, 31; in Galveston battle, 17–20; in
   Gettysburg campaign, 47–48; in New
   Mexico campaign, 8; in Red River cam-
   paign, 51–54; in Sabine Pass fighting,
   22–27; reaction to surrender, 61
Texas: annexation, 1; Declaration of
   Independence, 1; deserters in, 43–46;
   frontier, 47–49; Historical Commission,
   7, historical markers, 3, 7, 15, 21, 26, 36,
   43, 48, 55, 61; Parks and Wildlife
   Department, 25; Partisan Rangers, 40, 42;
   recruiting of troops, 5–6, 13; refugees in,
   32–33; regiments at Shiloh, 9; secession,
   1–2; shortages in, 31–32; State Cemetary,
   3; State Library, Archives Division, 63;
   support for Confederacy, 44; unionists
   in, 35–43; women in, 44–45
Third Louisiana Infantry: 7
Third Texas Cavalry: 7, 8
Third Texas Infantry: 27
Thirty-fourth Texas Cavalry: 60
Throckmorton, James W.: 35, 36, 67n
Tonkawas: 48
trade: through Mexico, 33
Trans-Mississippi Department: 34, 51, 59, 62
Travis County: 6
"Treue Der Union" ("Loyalty to the Union"):
   43
Truehart family papers: 63
Twentieth Texas Infantry: 17, 27
Twenty-seventh Texas Cavalry: vi
Twenty-sixth Texas Cavalry: 17

Twenty-third Texas Cavalry: 27
Twiggs, David E: 3
Tyler, Texas: 6, 32, 54, 55

U

Uncle Ben: 21, 24
unionists: 35–43
Union Loyal League: 40
United States Second Cavalry: 9
Ute scouts: 48

V

Valverde, battle of: 8, 65
Van Buren, Martin: 39
Van Dorn, Earl: 8
Velasco, Texas. 33
Velocity: 21
Vicksburg, campaign of 22, 65
Virginia: 22, 31, 32, 56
Virginia Point: 31
Vosburg, Sarah: 45

W

Waco, Texas: 6
Wainwright, Jonathan M.: 19
Walker, John C.: 52
Walker's Texas Division: 52–54
Washington, D.C.: 39, 40
Waul, Thomas N.: 52
weapons: 6
Webster, John J.: 36
Weitzel, Godfrey: 22
Wells, Angelica: 39
Westfield: 20–21
Wharton, John A.: 10, 54, 67; bust of, 3
Wharton's cavalry division: 54–55, 56
Whitfield, John W.: 8
Whitmore, George: 37
Wigfall, Louis T.: 55
Wilderness, campaign of: 56–57
Wilson's Creek, battle of: 7, 64
Wise County: 43
women: 44–45

Y

Yellow Bayou, battle of: 54
yellow fever: 25
Young, William C.: 7, 8, 36
Young, William H.: 57
Young County: 47, 48

ABOUT THE AUTHOR

Ralph A. Wooster is a semi-retired professor of history at Lamar University, Beaumont. An award-winning teacher and scholar, he is past president of the Texas State Historical Association and is the author and editor of numerous articles and books, including *Lone Star Blue and Gray: Essays on Texas in the Civil War* and *Texas and Texans in the Civil War*